Poem of the End

Also by Marina Tsvetaeva from Shearsman Books

Milestones
After Russia (The First Notebook)
After Russia (The Second Notebook)
Youthful Verses

(all translated by Christopher Whyte)

Marina Tsvetaeva

Poem of the End
and other narrative poems

Translated from Russian by
Nina Kossman

Shearsman Books

Published in the United Kingdom in 2021 by
Shearsman Books Ltd
PO Box 4239
Swindon
SN3 9FN

Shearsman Books Ltd Registered Office
30–31 St. James Place, Mangotsfield, Bristol BS16 9JB
(this address not for correspondence)

www.shearsman.com

ISBN 978-1-84861-778-0

Translations copyright © Nina Kossman, 1998, 2021.
Preface copyright © Laura Weeks, 1998.

The right of Nina Kossman to be identified as the translator of this work has been asserted by her in accordance with the Copyrights, Designs and Patents Act of 1988.
All rights reserved.

The translations in this volume first appeared in
Poem of the End: Selected Narrative and Lyrical Poems
(Ardis Publishers, Woodstock and New York, NY, 1998;
2nd edition, The Overlook Press, New York, NY, 2009).

CONTENTS

| | Translator's Note | 7 |
| | Introduction | 9 |

22	НА КРАСНОМ КОНЕ / On a Red Steed	23
36	ПОЭМА ГОРЫ / Poem of the Mountain	37
54	ПОЭМА КОНЦА / Poem of the End	55
108	ПОПЫТКА КОМНАТЫ / An Attempt at a Room	109
124	НОВОГОДНЕЕ / New Year's Greetings	125
136	ПОЭМА ВОЗДУХА / Poem of the Air	137

| | Notes | 158 |

TRANSLATOR'S NOTE

Transplanting poems from one language into another is a notoriously difficult task – in Tsvetaeva's case bewilderingly so. Tsvetaeva, who practically rebuilt Russian syntax for her own use, nevertheless wrote in rhyme and meter. Russian, an inflected language, is especially well suited to it, and Russian poets have continued writing in rhyme up to the present day, whereas modern English poetry in rhyme is a distinct subcategory. So besides the difficulty of translating a Russian rhymed poem into English rhyme that would create the same effect, there is the additional problem of what rhyme and meter *per se* suggest to readers in different cultures. Tsvetaeva's intensity, which in Russian perfectly agrees with her pattern of rhyme and rhythm, is bound to be lost whenever rhyme and meter become a translator's primary concern. In an earlier book of Tsvetaeva translations, *In the Inmost Hour of the Soul,* I included a few metrically translated poems. However, I keep only one such poem here. My aim was to carry the energy of the original poem into the English, to create poems that could stand on their own in English as far as possible, without losing either content or rhythm.

But to speak of Tsvetaeva's poetry only in technical terms would be to do her a great injustice. Though considered an extremely language-conscious poet, Tsvetaeva herself did not see language as a goal: to her it was an obstacle to overcome. In a letter to Rilke she wrote:

> Goethe says somewhere that one can't create anything worthwhile in a foreign language, yet I've always thought this was wrong… What is writing poetry but translating, from a native [i.e., inner-N.K.] tongue to a foreign one? – whether French or German doesn't make any difference… For that reason I don't understand why people speak of French, Russian, etc., poets. A poet may write in French and yet not be a French poet… I'm not a Russian poet and am always puzzled when I'm seen as one. This is just why one becomes a poet (if it were possible to become one, if one were not born a poet!) – in order not to be French, Russian, etc., in order to be all of them. In other words, one is a poet because one is not French. Nationality-the shutting out and shutting in. Orpheus bursts nationality, or extends its boundaries so far and wide that all (the bygone and the living) are included in it.'

Preoccupation with form for its own sake, was, in Tsvetaeva's eyes, an offense against "the elements," and she vehemently resisted being labelled a formal innovator. She praised Pasternak for bringing "...not a new form but a new essence, and consequently a new form." She twisted language not because she enjoyed word games for their own sake but because the task she set for herself demanded it: "My difficulty (in writing poems and maybe for others-in understanding them) is in the impossibility of my aim ... with words (that is, with meanings) to express a moan: ah-ah-ah.'? Marina Tsvetaeva was an outsider and a mythmaker, a rebel against every imaginable pretence who addressed herself "above heads – to God." She is best listened to as a sibyl (*sivilla*) – one of her favourite personas – and no one has claimed that sibyls are always easy to understand.

She was also a vulnerable human being who lived a terribly difficult, lonely, and, from what we know, uncompromising life:

> I am a person skinned alive, while all of you have armour. You all have your art, social issues, friendships, diversions, family, duty. I, deep down, have NOTHING. It all falls off like the skin and under the skin-Jiving flesh or fire: me, Psyche. I do not fit into any form, not even the simplest form of my poems.'

My hope is that these translations will carry through at least some of that living flesh, that fire.

I am indebted to Laura Weeks for her detailed and very useful suggestions for the earlier versions of the five *poemas*. And, last but not least, to Andrew Newcomb, without whose help and support these translations would not have been what they are.

Nina Kossman

NOTES

1. From Tsvetaeva's letter to Rilke, July 6, 1926.
2. From Tsvetaeva's diary, October 8, 1940.
3. From Tsvetaeva's letter to Alexandr Bakhrakh, September 10, 1923
    (*Literaturnoe obozrenie,* No. 10, p. 104, 1991).

INTRODUCTION

Marina Tsvetaeva is widely acclaimed as one of the great Russian poets of the twentieth century. Her path to fame, however, was not the meteor's or comet's path she once claimed for all poets, but more that of the Biblical measure of leaven, which lay hidden until the bread suddenly doubled in size. At the time of her "rediscovery" in the 1960s, she was the property of a privileged few – small scattered groups of scholars and poetry lovers who were acquainted with a fraction of her total work, and a biography full of palpable gaps.[1] In the '80s the gaps in her biography were filled in, the amount of available material doubled, and so did her audience. At this time she was firmly re-established in her native land, and emerged on the world stage as well, thanks to translations of her poetry into English, French, Italian and German.

The present volume, compiled and translated by Nina Kossman, is devoted to Tsvetaeva's long quasi-narrative poems or *poemy* – a genre unique to Russian literature. A brief comparison of the lyric poem and the *poema* is in order, first because English-speaking readers who are already acquainted with Tsvetaeva's lyric poetry may be less familiar with her mastery of the longer genre, and secondly, because her *poemy* are notoriously difficult to grasp.

Part of the difficulty lies in their length. Although the original epic-heroic subject matter has long disappeared from the *poema*, the reader still has to contend with its greater length. For the poet, the *poema*'s length translates into the question of sustained creativity. Tsvetaeva once wrote to her Czech friend and benefactress, Anna Teskova, that only a master could produce a *poema*, because a single lyrical impulse might yield a stanza, or at most, a block of 10-12 lines in finished form. Yet for Tsvetaeva, who was, in Boris Pasternak's words, an extraordinarily deep-chested singer (one who does not run out of breath over very long phrases), sustaining the lyrical moment does not seem to have presented a challenge. It was the gaps between the lyrical bursts that she feared. As she wrote to Pasternak,

> Lyric poems … are separate moments of *one* movement: a movement in segments … A lyric is a dotted line. From afar it looks solid, black, but if you look closely, it's all in the gaps between the dots – airless space, death. And you die from poem to poem.

In a book (a novel, a *poema,* even an article) this is not so – they have their own rules. A book doesn't want to discard its author, the people-fates-souls about which you write want to live, and they want to live further, each day more, they don't want to end. (Letter of 11 February 1923)[2]

Pursuing the distinction between Tsvetaeva's short lyric poems and her *poemy,* Olga Peters Hasty concludes that it lies in the relationship of the part to the whole.[3] The short lyrics point both forward and backward to the poems that flank them chronologically. The *poema* points inward to its own internal centre of gravity. To borrow a figure from Tsvetaeva's own 'Poets with a History and Poets without a History,' the one is an arrow loosed into infinity, the other a closed circle. Because of the *poemy's* more obvious sense of closure, Hasty refers to them as "the stones around which the stream of Cvetaeva's lyric verse flows" (Hasty, 1988, 395). Thus, from the point of view of their creator, the *poemy* are at once more difficult and more satisfying than the short lyric poem. They have a longer life (see above, "they don't want to end"), and they have the ability to heal the wound or gap between each short lyric and the next. In Hastys words,

> Cvetaeva regards the intervals between lyric poems as wounds – tears in that organic whole they compromise. Each completion of a poem creates at the same time a gap, a wound which must be healed by the opening of the following poem (Hasty, 394).

The *poema,* by contrast, has the ability to stitch these rips in the seam of the self. Not for nothing does the heroine of Tsvetaeva's *The Poem of the End* tell the hero, "I have sewn up your entire life in one night," referring both to the ending of their unhappy love affair, and to completion of the *poema* itself.

Yet despite the formal difference between the lyric poem and the *poema,* their function remains the same – to explore certain areas of emotional experience, certain thematic concerns. In another letter to Teskova, Tsvetaeva described the nature of her creativity as a whirlpool: "I cannot confine myself to one poem – with me they come in families, cycles, almost like a funnel or even a whirlpool into which I tumble" (Letter of 24 November 1933).[4] Extrapolating one step further, we might say that the *poema* is the next stage after the cycle. The same lyrical impulse that yields a single poem, then a cluster of related poems or a cycle, spills over into the long form before it finally falls silent. In light of Tsvetaeva's statement about the level of mastery needed to create the long form, we might also conclude that each *poema* is a statement of mastery marking the end of a certain stage of development of Tsvetaeva the poet. The Russian for this kind of watershed marking the boundaries between the stages in an artist's growth is *etapnyi*, and Tsvetaeva's *poemy* are *etapnye* in the highest sense of the Russian word, which is why they most often were published separately. To extend Olga Peters Hasty's metaphor, they are not just stones, but milestones, after which the river takes a sharp bend.

A look at the *poemy* in their chronological clusters supports this theory. Tsvetaeva's first mature collection of lyric poetry, *Milestones (Versty (I))* not only marked the emergence of a major voice in Russian poetry, it demonstrated a very high level of mastery of the so-called *style Russe*, that is, the tropes and diction borrowed from Russian folk heritage. Tsvetaeva would continue to explore this vein over the next four years (1916–20) in the first half of the collection *Milestones (Versty (II))*, and in the collection dedicated to the "heroic defeat" of the White Army, *The Swans' Camp (Lebedinyi stan)*. At the culmination of this period come five *poemy*, all of them written in the period 1920–22, all of them written in this vein. Three of them draw their plots directly from Alexander Afanasiev's collection of Russian fairy tales: *The King-Maiden (Tsar' devitsa* [1920]), *Side Streets (Pereulochki* [1922]), and *The Swain (Molodets* [1922]). Another, the unfinished *Egorushka* (1920–21), draws on popular legend, in this case the folk version of St. George – hero, dragon-slayer and patron saint of Moscow.

Naturally, these popular legends are not transmitted whole, but are creatively deformed by Tsvetaeva to brilliant effect. Among the purely Tsvetaevan features in *The King-Maiden*, we find an incestuous relationship between stepmother and stepson, a force of nature (the wind) elevated to the level of a *dramatis persona*, and a completely unexpected (perhaps even for Tsvetaeva herself) peasant rebellion that erupts in the *poema*'s final pages. The mystical union-in-death of the King-Maiden and her Prince is another Tsvetaevan trademark which is replayed in *The Swain*. Abandoning Afanasiev's original plot, *The Swain* concludes with the mystical union-in-death and ascension of Marusia and her vampire lover. *On a Red Steed*, also written in this period, is something of an exception, as it does not borrow its plot ready-made from any source. Instead, Tsvetaeva uses the diction of folklore to convey a highly personal experience of art and the artist.

The Ratcatcher (Krysolov), a creative reworking of the legend of *The Pied Piper of Hamlin*, written in emigration between March and November of 1925, is unquestionably a masterpiece of world literature. It also represents the summation of all the *poemy* to this point. It features a popular fairytale plot told in folkloric diction heavily laced with irony, and has as its central issue an examination of the role of the artist in society. It even features a brief excursis into history such as occurred in *The King-Maiden*. Here, an invasion of rats symbolizes the October Revolution of 1917.

In 1926, Tsvetaeva would abandon the language of folklore and move on to more metaphysical themes. The *poemy* she produced in 1926 and 1927 are ostensibly a form of personal letter addressed to a significant correspondent in her life, but they are in fact philosophical meditations in the neoclassical tradition – meditations on time, space and the nature of God, such as her predecessors Mikhail Lermontov and Gavrila Derzhavin wrote. They are also occasional verse in the eighteenth-century sense: her *New Year's Greetings* (*Novogodnee* [1927]) was written to mark the death of Rainer Maria Rilke, and *Poem of the Air (Poema vozdukha)* was written to celebrate Lindbergh's first nonstop transatlantic flight (May 20-21, 1927). Like the earlier chronological cluster, these *poemy* demonstrate Tsvetaeva's mastery of the themes treated in her short lyric poems of 1922–25, all of which were included in her last published collection of verse, *After Russia* (*Posle Rossii*). There she explored such abstractions as time, immortality and the nature of God.

From 1927 until her return to the Soviet Union in 1939, Tsvetaeva turned increasingly to history and to the poet's place as a chronicler of history. Her own personal history was recorded in her brilliant autobiographical prose sketches. This period also yielded the short lyric poems 'Homeland' (*Rodina*) and 'To Our Fathers' (*Ottsam*), as well as *poemy* on historical and political themes: *The Red Bull Calf* (*Krasnyi bychok* [1928]), an unfinished *poema* about the Tsar's family, and *Perekop* (1939), an account of the last stand of the White Army in the Civil War on the isthmus of Perekop. In their preoccupation with history, Tsvetaeva's *poemy* mirror the concerns of her own generation as well as the development of the *poema* as a genre. In the thirties and forties, the *poema* moved away from the exploration of intense personal experiences to broader, more impersonal themes, especially history: witness Pasternak's *Spektorsky* and Anna Akhmatova's *Poem Without a Hero (Poema bez geroia)*.

§ § §

The six works chosen by Nina Kossman for this collection are an excellent introduction to Tsvetaeva's *poemy*. Appearing here, several for the first time, in a sensitive and accurate English translation, they include selections from the first two chronological groups: the early period inspired by Russian folklore, and the middle period devoted to philosophical meditations. The first *poema, On a Red Steed,* shows Tsvetaeva at her most lyrical-Romantic. The next two, *The Poem of the Mountain* and *The Poem of the End,* demonstrate her mastery of the lyrical-confessional mode. The next three *poemy, Attempt at a Room, New Year's Greetings,* and *Poem of the Air,* introduce readers to Tsvetaeva in the '20s, when she was at the height of her powers as a poet, especially in the haunting *New Year's Greetings,* where as Joseph Brodsky says, she proved "[her soul] had nothing left to learn from literature, not even from Rilke."[5]

The *poema On a Red Steed* appears here in its abbreviated form, as published in the collection *Psyche. Romance. (Psikheia. Romantika,* 1923). It first appeared at the end of the collection *Separation (Razluka,* 1922) bearing a dedication to Anna Akhmatova. The original dedication is revealing of the *poema*'s intent. This is a tale of art and the artist, a celebration of Tsvetaeva's carefully cultivated masculine muse. Although Tsvetaeva's daughter later maintained that the mysterious male muse is Tsvetaeva's idol, Alexander Blok, it is clearly Tsvetaeva's response to Akhmatova, the reigning female voice in twentieth-century Russian poetry. This is the motivation behind the heroine's cry, "I need no women's tresses. I need no red beads," beads and tresses being Akhmatova's trademarks.

Not only is the *poema* a rejection of Akhmatova's patently feminine muse, it is a rejection of femaleness itself. The ritual exorcism of femaleness takes place in successive stages. In the longer version, the powerful masculine muse forces the heroine in three separate episodes to give up an emblem of her femaleness: the little girl gives up her doll; the young woman gives up her lover; the mature woman gives up her child.

The losses, however, are more than compensated by the heroine's transformation from Woman Warrior to poet. In the penultimate section, the muse drives his spear into the heroine's heart, an act which echoes the final meeting of the King-Maiden and her prince. There the Woman Warrior drove her sword into her side in order to join her lover in a bodiless spiritual union. In *On a Red Steed* that symbolic wound becomes the stigmata initiating the heroine into the mysteries of art. Furthermore, the Warrior Poet's final vision has definite affinities with Christian mysticism. Compare the stabbing of the heroine's heart with a spear of light to the vision of St. Teresa de Ávila immortalized by Bernini. Compare the muse's possession of the heroine to the Catholic doctrine of the nun (i.e., one who has renounced Eros) as the bride of Christ. Finally, it may be that in conquering Eros, by allowing the beloved objects to be destroyed, the heroine has succeeded in transforming Eros into Agape.

The next two *poemy*, the *Poem of the Mountain* (*Poema gory*) and the *Poem of the End* (*Poema kontsa*) do not fall neatly into the chronological categories of folklore or metaphysics. They do, however, expand on two of the central features of *On a Red Steed:* the religious imagery, and the confessional mode. This last especially is in keeping with the changing nature of the *poema,* which early in this century had abandoned the nineteenth-century heroic-epic model to focus instead on a single intense emotional experience. The experience Tsvetaeva here records is the end of her affair with Konstantin Rodzevich.

Konstantin Rodzevich was a former officer in the White Army, a friend of Tsvetaeva's husband and a fellow student at Charles University. Their affair lasted from September to December of 1923. While Tsvetaeva was no stranger to extramarital attachments, this affair, like her earlier affair with Sophia Pamok, threatened to rupture her marriage. She wrote *Poem of the Mountain* in January of 1924, and *Poem of the End* from February to June of 1924.

In a letter to Pasternak, Tsvetaeva described the two *poemy* as one, "only the *Poem of the Mountain* is earlier, and is the masculine aspect … written in the first heat, beginning right off on the highest note" (Letter of 26 May 1926). If the imagery in *On a Red Steed* was predominantly borrowed from Christian mysticism, the poet's voice here has the angry quality of an Old Testament prophet. Old Testament imagery abounds: Jehovah, Hagar, Sinai, the seventh commandment, the Garden of Eden. At the same time, the actual description of the lovers is fleeting, almost impersonal. The lovers take second place to a diatribe against philistines who profane the sacred places of art.

The *Poem of the End,* by contrast, is the female voice: "an outburst of female grief, streaming tears, I when I lie down – not the same I when I wake up. *The Poem of the Mountain* is the mountain seen from another mountain. *The Poem of the End* is the mountain on me. I am under it." (Letter of 26 May) Yet underneath Tsvetaeva's mountain, at the heart of her grief, lies steel. *The Poem of the End* is a brilliant exposition of the battle of the sexes, replete with images of duelling and battle. The meeting of the lovers at the lamp post resembles nothing so much as the meeting of two opponents at the appointed hour for a duel, from the hero's exaggerated politeness ("in every eyelash – a challenge") to his strangely formal bow mimicking the opening of a fencing match. This opening is followed by images of bared swords, gunpowder, a strung bow, the drum-roll of battle and culminates in an extended reference to a duel. These images gradually dissolve as the couple begins their journey backward in time to happier days, and resolve when the heroine has won the pearl of pearls (his tear in her hand) and the song of songs (the writing of the *poema*).

Tsvetaeva and Rodzevich's affair played itself out against the backdrop of the outskirts of Prague, and the landmarks are crucial to an understanding of the *poema:* the factories, cafés, side-streets, the bridge across the river Vltava, and of course the hill or "Mountain" – Petrshin Kholm in the Smikhov region. Tsvetaeva makes strategic use of these landmarks to create a spatial arrangement of near-perfect symmetry. The lamppost and the finger of fate appear in canto 1 and again in canto 11. The river embankment appears in canto 3 and again in canto 7. The cafe in canto 4 is echoed by the appearance of the coffee shop/milk bar in 10. Only the bridge, that liminal space between life and death, is left alone at the centre of the *poema*.

Taking his cue from an observation Tsvetaeva made in her working notebooks, Tomas Venclova has identified the *poema*'s spatial arrangement as an enactment of the stations of the cross.[6] Readers will recognize the lovers' last evening transformed into a kind of Last Supper, the kiss of betrayal, the three episodes of falling (here the heroine "clings to the water's edge" to prevent herself from falling), the crucifixion on the Mount. Since the two *poemy* are born of a single impulse, Venclova concludes that the *Poem of the Mountain* is an enactment of the Old Testament (the expulsion from Eden, the receiving of God's voice on Sinai, and so on) while the *Poem of the End* is an enactment of the New Testament passion. Once again we see the role of the *poema* as a summation. The predominant source of imagery in the chronologically related collection *After Russia* is also Biblical.

The next three *poemy* belong to the period of philosophical meditations. The first, *Attempt at a Room (Popytka komnaty)*, was written in 1926 and addressed to Boris Pasternak. Tsvetaeva and Pasternak had crossed paths at least twice in Moscow before she left Russia to join her husband in emigration, but it was not until the summer of 1922 that they came to know each other as poets. While still in Berlin, that strange halfway house of Russian emigration in the twenties, Tsvetaeva received a letter from Pasternak full of ecstasy over her recent poetry. She quickly devoured his *My Sister-Life* and responded no less ecstatically. Thus began an intense epistolary affair that continually threatened to erupt into something more physical, as Pasternak more than once offered to abandon everything to be able to join her, while Tsvetaeva continually chose to fence him off.

Attempt at a Room was written in June of 1926 while Tsvetaeva was vacationing in St. Gilles sur Vie. It is an attempt to communicate with Pasternak over the enormous distance separating them, to create a dream meeting in another dimension. Tsvetaeva believed in what today might be termed "out of body" experiences, especially dream meetings, which she claimed were more real and satisfying than actual meetings in the flesh, where an individual's soul is hidden behind the wall of his body. "Another person's body is a wall!" Tsvetaeva once wrote to her mentor, Max Voloshin, "It prevents one from seeing his soul. Oh, how I hate that wall!"[7]

On another level, it is an attempt to conquer space by the power of language. The hypothetical room is actually a space in the brain, which is cleared and prepared as carefully as any housewife getting ready for guests could wish. In the process of preparation, disturbing images arise associated with the fourth wall, which is consciously omitted from the room. As the poet deliberately turns her back on it, she assigns it a special status: it is a kind of window into another level of reality, and a conduit of creativity. At the same time, it is compared to the wall of a firing squad, a bayonet attack in the rear, and with Pushkin's fatal duel, as his second steps out of it to summon him to his death. In short, there is more than a hint of death, the most common means of leaving the body behind.

When Tsvetaeva had finished *Attempt at a Room,* she was displeased by its abstractness. She wrote to Pasternak, "The poem about you and me ... turned out to be about me and him. *Every line of it*" (Letter of 9 February 1927). "Him" in this case was Rainer Maria Rilke. Pasternak's father had met Rilke during the latter's trips to Russia in the early 1900s. He took the occasion of Rilke's fiftieth birthday to renew their acquaintance by letter and to introduce Rilke to his son's work. Pasternak, in turn, introduced Rilke to "a wonderful Russian poet," Marina Tsvetaeva. Throughout 1926 the three poets corresponded – a correspondence resembling a conversation on Olympus for the loftiness of ideas, the intensity of its lyricism, and the density of its language (with occasional lapses into unintelligibility). Rilke was something of a shrine for Tsvetaeva and Pasternak: they worshipped him and the German lyrical tradition he stood for. They even made plans to visit him, but unknown to them, he was already dying of leukaemia. Tsvetaeva in fact was awaiting a response to her last letter when she received the news. The bearer was the critic Mark Slonim, a longtime friend and supporter, who had stopped by to invite her to celebrate New Year's Eve at the Alcazar. In passing he mentioned that Rilke had died two days before in a sanatorium in Switzerland.

Tsvetaeva's tribute to Rilke, *New Year's Greetings* (*Novogodnee*, [19271]), is a hauntingly beautiful requiem that bursts asunder the confines of the *poema*. Ostensibly in the form of a personal letter, it combines elements of the elegy, the lament and the love lyric. It is also more than a tribute to Rilke. If *Attempt at a Room* was an attempt to conquer space, *New Year's Greetings* is an attempt to conquer death. (Tsvetaeva herself wrote to Teskova that it was coloured by Rilke's death and the deaths of two others: her daughter's French teacher and a little Russian émigré boy they knew.) It is an exploration of life after death, for both Rilke and Tsvetaeva herself are eminently present. It is a most astonishing piece of work, even for those who are prepared for Tsvetaeva's peculiar double vision. From her earliest poems she projected visions of herself seeing her own body laid out for burial or addressing a passer-by after her own death, but here she surpasses herself. As Brodsky points out in his sensitive analysis of the *poema*, the shock lies in the location of the poet's "I" (Brodsky, 1988). If from her imaginary vantage point Tsvetaeva observes Rilke observing his newly abandoned body, or Rilke observing the earth, now shrunken to the size of a distant star, where must Tsvetaeva be, if not further out in time and space than Rilke?

Brodsky also points out that a large part of the *poema's* pathos is created by the child's eye view of the universe Tsvetaeva espouses. Tsvetaeva loved Rilke because German (and especially German Romantic poetry) was an intimate part of her childhood, and childhood experiences provide some of the *poema's* most striking imagery. The series of questions she poses to Rilke are childlike in their insistence, but the answers are not childish: heaven as an amphitheatre; heaven as a landscape without tourists; God as a growing baobab tree. What Tsvetaeva creates in her *New Year's Greetings* is an entirely original picture of the universe.

The last *poema* from this period, *Poem of the Air (Poema Vozdukha* [1927]), was written to celebrate Lindbergh's nonstop transatlantic flight, but that of course was only the external pretext. It is, to say the least, a difficult poem; Brodsky describes it as "hieroglyphic." Like the "first air" it describes, it is dense, opaque. Nor is it necessarily more comprehensible to a native speaker of Russian, or a poet of Tsvetaeva's own stature. Akhmatova, writing in her diary in the sixties, remarked, "Marina has retreated into transrational language (*zaum*). Look at her *Poema vozdukha* (*Poem of the Air*)."[8]

One way of reading the *poema* is as a continuation of *New Year's Greetings*, that is, a further exploration of the afterlife, or as Anatoly Naiman calls it, "the posthumous journey of the hero's soul" (Naiman, 1994, 101). If in *New Year's Greetings* Tsvetaeva's heaven as a series of terraces had a vaguely Dantean shape to it, here we get a very Dantean guided tour through the empyrean, layer by layer.

The emphasis on purely physical sensations in *Poem of the Air* gives rise to the possibility of another reading, however. There is a sense of joyful exuberance as the poet is liberated in successive stages from the confines of existence: from the senses, from sickness, from gravity, from the earth itself. But this joyful process is overshadowed by images of struggle: the resistance of the rye fields, the battering of the fragile airplane in the lower air, the scythe-like winnowing of the upper air, the thrashing of an epileptic fit, and finally, the gasping of a fish out of water. Tsvetaeva has chosen to give equal weight to the sensations of breathing, and to the gaps between breaths, and as she herself notes, "those pauses aren't sweet, they are transfers from the local into the interspatial" – pauses that leave one literally gasping for air. Thus, instead of merely a joyful "escape from earth," we have a physical description of the soul at the exact moment of leaving the body, as startling and intimate as Tolstoy's *Death of Ivan Ilyich*. Both Ivan Ilyich in his black bag and Tsvetaeva's persona in the upper air experience a gradual suffocation. Naiman reads this gradual suffocation as a metaphor for the poet's existence. The air is the poet's otherworldly atmosphere. When it loses its resonance and dries up, the poet suffocates: "Marina suffocated like a sea creature on the shore, cast out of her native element" (Naiman, 1994, 105).

However we read the *poema*, it is clear that Tsvetaeva held great store by it and felt compelled to share it with others. When she met Akhmatova after her return to the Soviet Union, she copied out *Poem of the Air* for her. Two days before her death, she found herself in the home of the Schneiders, people who loved her poetry and sympathized with her plight. When asked to recite some of her newer things, she chose first "Homesickness" (*Toska po rodine*), then *Poem of the Air*. No one who heard her recite realized that she had succeeded in describing the thing she feared: "the gaps between the dots – airless space, death."

Laura Weeks

NOTES

1. There is by now an impressive list of biographies of Tsvetaeva in English. In addition to Viktoria Schweitzer's massive opus, which has now been translated (Viktoria Schweitzer, *Tsvetaeva* [London: Harper Collins, 1992]), readers may choose from a variety of approaches to Tsvetaeva's life: Lily Feiler, *Marina Tsvetaeva. The Double Beat of Heaven and Hell* (Durham, NC: Duke University Press, 1994); Elaine Feinstein, *A Captive Lion. The Life of Marina Tsvetaeva* (London: Hutchinson, 1987); Simon Karlinsky, *Marina Tsvetaeva. The Woman, Her World and Her Poetry* (Cambridge: Cambridge University Press, 1985); Jane A. Taubman, *A Life Through Poetry: Marina Tsvetaeva's Lyric Diary* (Ohio: Slavica Publishers 1988).
2. Marina Tsvetaeva, *Neizdannye pis'ma* (Paris: YMCA, 1971), 278-79. The English translation appears in Jane Taubman, op. cit., 211.
3. Olga Peters Hasty, "Poema vs. Cycle in Cvetaeva's Definition of Lyric Verse," *Slavic and East European Journal*, 32, 3, 1988.
4. Marina Tsvetaeva, *Pis'ma k A. Teskovoi* (Jerusalem: Versty, 1982), 105. The translation is mine.

NARRATIVE POEMS

НА КРАСНОМ КОНЕ

Не Муза, не Муза
Над бедною люлькой
Мне пела, за ручку водила.
Не Муза холодные руки мне грела,
Горячие веки студила.
Вихор ото лба отводила – не Муза,
В большие поля уводила – не Муза.

Не Муза, не черные косы, не бусы,
Не басни, – всего два крыла светлорусых
– Коротких – над бровью крылатой.
Стан в латах.
Султан.

К устам не клонился,
На сон не крестил.
О сломанной кукле
Со мной не грустил.
Всех птиц моих – на свободу
Пускал – и потом – не жалея шпор,
На красном коне – промеж синих гор
Гремящего ледохода!

§

Пожарные! – Широкий крик!
Как зарево широкий – крик!
Пожарные! – Душа горит!
Не наш ли дом горит?!

Сполòшный колокол гремит,
Качай-раскачивай язык,
Сполòшный колокол! – Велик
Пожар! – Душа горит!

ON A RED STEED

No Muse, no Muse
Sang over my shabby
Cradle, or took me by the hand.
No muse warmed my cold hands in her own,
Or cooled my burning eyelids:
No Muse brushed the strands from my brow,
And led me into the open fields.

No Muse, no black braids, no beads,
No fables – just two wings of light hair,
Cut short over winged brows:
A man in armour.
A horsehair plume.

He did not bow towards my lips,
He did not bless me at bedtime.
He did not grieve with me
Over a broken doll.
He set all my birds free
Then – not sparing his spurs,
Rode a red steed – through the blue mountains
Of a thundering ice-flow.

§

Firemen! – A wide-mouthed shout!
A shout wide as a blaze!
Firemen! – A soul on fire!
Is that our house on fire?

The bell tolls ceaselessly.
Swing-toll your tongue,
Ceaseless bell! – The fire is
Vast. – A soul on fire!

Пляша от страшной красоты,
На красных факелов жгуты
Рукоплещу, – кричу – свищу –
Рычу – искры мечу.

Кто вынес? – Кто сквозь гром и чад
Орлом восхитил? – Не очнусь!
Рубашка – длинная – до пят
На мне – и нитка бус.

Вой пламени, стекольный лязг...
У каждого – заместо глаз –
Два зарева! – Полет перин!
Горим! Горим! Горим!

Трещи, тысячелетний ларь!
Пылай, накопленная кладь!
Мой дом – над всеми государь,
Мне нечего желать.

– Пожарные! – Крепчай, Петух!
Грянь в раззолоченные лбы!
Чтобы пожар не тух, не тух!
Чтоб рухнули столбы!

Что это – вдруг – рухнуло – вдруг?
Это не столб – рухнул!
Бешеный всплеск маленьких рук
В небо – и крик: – Кукла!

Кто это – вслед – скоком гоня
Взор мне метнул – властный?
Кто это – вслед – скоком с коня
Красного – в дом – красный?!

Крик – и перекричавший всех
Крик. – Громовой удар.

Dancing from the terrible beauty,
Plaits of flame on red torches…
I clang – blare – clap,
I snarl, I shoot sparks.

Who carried me out? Who, through the rumble and fumes,
Like an eagle, carried me out? I can't come to!
A long gown hangs on me
And a string of beads.

The roaring fire, the clanging glass…
Instead of eyes, in each face –
Two flames. Featherbeds flying.
Fire! Fire! Fire!

Split open, thousand-year-old coffers!
Burn, hoarded wealth!
My house is lord over all,
I want for nothing.

Firemen! – Spread, red-winged flame!
Shine on gilded foreheads.
Let the fire never die, never die.
Let the pillars crash.

What – suddenly – what collapsed?
That was no pillar crashing.
A wild clasping of small hands
And a shout – up to the sky: "The doll!"

Who was it, from his plunging steed,
Threw after me an imperious glance?
Who, leaping off his red steed,
Entered the red house?

A shout – and louder still
A shout. A thunder-clap.

Вздымая куклу, как доспех,
Встает, как сам Пожар.

Как Царь меж огненных зыбей
Встает, сдвигает бровь.
– Я спас ее тебе, – разбей!
Освободи Любовь!

§

Что это вдруг – рухнуло? – Нет,
Это не мир – рухнул!
То две руки – конному – вслед
Девочка – без – куклы.

§

Февраль. Кривые дороги.
В полях – метель.
Метет большие дороги
Ветрòв – артель.

То вскачь по хребтам наклонным,
То снова круть.
За красным, за красным конным
Всё тот же путь.

То – вот он! рукой достанешь!
Как дразнит: Тронь!
Безумные руки тянешь,
И снегом – конь.

Султан ли – в глазах – косматый,
Аль так – ветла?
Эй, рук не складайте, сваты!
Мети, ветра!

Holding the doll aloft like armour,
He rises up like the Fire itself.

Kinglike, among fiery ripples,
He rises up, his brow knit.
– I've saved it for you. Now break it!
Set your love free.

§

What – suddenly – what collapsed?
No, it's not the world collapsing.
Reaching after the horseman – the empty hands
Of the little girl with no doll.

§

February. Winding roads.
A snowstorm in the fields.
An alliance of winds
Sweeps the big roads.

Now galloping down the sloping hills,
Now mounting upwards.
The same road stretches
Behind the red horseman.

Here he is! Within reach!
How he teases: Touch me!
You stretch your hands wildly,
But instead of the horse – snow.

Is that his shaggy horsehair plume
In his eyes – or some branch?
No rest for you, matchmakers!
Sweep on, winds.

Мети, громозди пороги –
Превыше скал,
Чтоб конь его крутоногий
Как вкопан – стал.

И внемлют ветра – и стоном
В ответ на стон.
Торопится красным гоном
Мой конный сон.

Косматых воскрылий взлеты,
Аль так – ветла?
Вздымайте, вздымайте метлы!
Держись, ветра!

А что ж это там за глыба
Всплывает – там?
Как будто бы вьюгой вздыблен
Стоглавый храм.

Конец и венец погоне!
Уж в лоб, треща,
Мне пламень подков, в ладони –
Уж край плаща!

На помощь, с мечом и громом,
Всех Воинств Царь! –
Но прядает конь – и громом
Взгремел в алтарь!

§

Стремлю, а за мною – сворой
Вся рать ветров.
Еще не остыл – по хорам –
Раскат подков.

Sweep, pile up on the thresholds –
Higher than cliffs.
Let his swift-legged horse
Stop dead.

The winds harken: moan
Echoing moan.
My horseback dream hastens,
Scudding red.

Are those his shaggy, upswept wings?
Or just some branch?
Lift up your brooms, trees!
Hold tight, winds!

Is that a boulder
Looming – or what?
As if the blizzard had built
A thousand-spired church.

At last the chase is crowned.
The fire of his horse's hooves
Licks at my face; my hands
Touch the edge of his cloak.

Help, with thunder and sword,
Tsar of all armies!
But the steed stirs and like thunder
Bolts at the altar!

§

I spur on; behind me –
The whole horde of winds.
In the choir-loft the thunder of hooves
Has not yet died down.

Как рокот Сорокоуста
Метель взмелась:
Престол опрокинут! – Пусто!
Как в землю сгас!

Стоните, стоните, стены!
Метель, ярись!
Померкло от конской пены
Сиянье риз.

Шатается купол. – Рухай,
Сонм сил и слав!
И рухает тело – руки
Крестом распяв.

§

Огромною битвой радуг –
Разлет лампад.
– Прими меня, чист и сладок,
За ны – распят.

Ревнивая длань, – твой праздник!
Прими огонь!
Но что – с высоты – за всадник,
И что за конь?

Доспехи на нем – как солнце...
– Полет крутой –
И прямо на грудь мне – конской
Встает пятой.

§

Гром первый по черепу – или лом
По черепу?! – Люди! Люди!

Like the rumble of Requiem,
The snowstorm revives.
The altar's upended. – Empty!
Vanished into the earth.

Weep, wall, wail!
Snowstorm, rage on!
The horse's foam dims
The radiance of chasubles.

The dome is trembling. – Fall,
Hosts of might and glory.
And the body falls, its arms
Spread-eagled, like a cross.

§

The rays of the icon-lamps
Scatter like great rainbows.
–Receive me, thou pure and sweet,
Crucified for us.

This – your feast, o jealous palm:
Receive this flame.
But who is that horseman from on high,
And what is that steed?

His armour is like the sun…
His flight, steep…
Onto my chest he places
His horse's hoof.

§

Is that thunder in the cranium – or
A crowbar to the skull?! – People! – People!

В сухую подушку вгрызаясь лбом,
Впервые сказать: Не любит!

Не любит! – Не надо мне женских кос!
Не любит! – Не надо мне красных бус!
Не любит! – Так я на коня вздымусь!
Не любит! – Вздымусь – до неба!

О дух моих дедов, взыграй с цепи!
Шатай вековые сосны!
О дух моих дедов – Эол ! – трепи
Мои золотые космы!

На белом коне впереди полков
Вперед под серебряный гром подков!
Посмотрим, посмотрим – в бою каков
Гордец на коне на красном!

Разломано небо! – Благой знак:
Заря кровянит шлем мой!
Солдаты! До неба – один шаг:
Законом зерна – в землю!

Вперед – через ров! – Сорвались? – Ряд
Другой – через ров! – Сорвались? – Вновь
Другой – через ров! – На снегу лат
Не знаю: заря? кровь?

Солдаты! Какого врага – бьем?
В груди холопок – жгуч,
И входит, и входит стальным копьем
Под левую грудь – луч.

§

И шепот: Такой я тебя желал!
И рокот: Такой я тебя избрал,

Grinding the dry pillow with my brow,
To say, for the first time: He loves me not!

Loves me not! – I need no women's tresses!
Loves me not! – I need no red beads!
Loves me not! – I will mount my steed!
Loves me not! And rise up to – the sky!

Ancestral spirit, shake off your chains!
Rattle the primeval pines!
Ancestral spirit, Aeolus!
Tousle my golden mane.

Leading my regiments, on a white steed,
With a silvery thunder of hooves – forward!
We shall see how he does in battle,
That braggart on the red steed.

The sky has broken. A good sign:
Dawn bloodies my helmet!
Soldiers! It's one step from here to heaven:
By the law of the grain you go – into the ground!

Forward! – Over the trench! – Fallen?
Next row – Over the trench! – Fallen?
Again – Over the trench! – Is that
Dawn on the snow-white armour? Blood?

Soldiers! What enemy are we fighting?
A burning chill invades my breast.
And piercing, piercing my heart like a lance,
A ray of light.

§

He whispers: "I wanted you like this:"
And rumbles: "I chose you like this,

Дитя моей страсти – сестра – брат –
Невеста во льду – лат!

Моя и ничья – до конца лет.
Я, руки воздев: Свет!
– Пребудешь? Не будешь ничья, – нет?
Я, рану зажав: Нет.

§

Не Муза, не Муза, – не бренные узы
Родства, – не твои путы,
О Дружба! – Не женской рукой, – лютой
Затянут на мне –
Узел.

Сей страшен союз. – В черноте рва
Лежу, – а Восход светел.
О кто невесомых моих два
Крыла за плечом –
Взвесил?

Немой соглядатай
Живых бурь –
Лежу – и слежу
Тени.

Доколе меня
Не умчит в лазурь
На красном коне –
Мой Гений!

13–17 января 1921 г.

Child of my passion – sister – brother
My bride in armour of ice.

Mine and no other's – forever."
I, raising my arms: "Light."
"You shall be no other's. You swear this?"
I, stanching my wound: "Yes."

§

No Muse, no Muse – not the frail ties
Of kinship – No, not your bonds,
O friendship! That was no woman's hand – a fierce one
Drew this knot tight
Around me.

A terrifying union. I lie
In the trench's darkness – while the dawn rises.
Oh, who suspended these
Two weightless wings
On my shoulders?

A silent spy
Of living storms
I lie – and I watch
Shadows.

Until I'm whirled
Off into the blue
On the red steed
By my genius!

Moscow, 1921

ПОЭМА ГОРЫ

> Liebster, Dich wunder!
> die Rede? Alle Scheidenden
> reden wie Trunkene und
> nehmen gerne sich festlich...
> Hölderlin

ПОСВЯЩЕНИЕ

Вздрогнешь – и горы с плеч,
И душа – горе.
Дай мне о горе спеть:
О моей горе!

Черной ни днесь, ни впредь
Не заткну дыры.
Дай мне о горе спеть
На верху горы.

1

Та гора была как грудь
Рекрута, снарядом сваленного.
Та гора хотела губ
Девственных, обряда свадебного

Требовала та гора.
– Океан в ушную раковину
Вдруг-ворвавшимся ура! –
Та гора гнала и ратовала.

Та гора была как гром!
Грудь, титанами разыгранная!
(Той горы последний дом
Помнишь – на исходе пригорода?)

POEM OF THE MOUNTAIN

> Liebster, Dich wunder!
> die Rede? Alle Scheidenden
> reden wie Trunkene und
> nehmen gerne sich festlich…
> Hölderlin

DEDICATION

A shudder – a load off my shoulders,
And my soul shoots up.
Let me sing of my mourning:
Of my mountain.

I cannot, now or ever,
Stop up this black hole.
Let me sing of my mourning
Atop the mountain.

1

The mountain was like the breast
Of a recruit cut down by shells.
The mountain craved virgin lips,
And marriage rites.

The mountain demanded these.
– An ocean rushing into the ears
Like a sudden hurrah! –
The mountain raced and wrestled.

The mountain was like thunder!
Flesh raffled off by Titans!
(Do you remember the last house
At the mountain's foot, at the suburb's edge?)

Та гора была – миры!
Бог за мир взымает дорого!

....

Горе началось с горы.
Та гора была над городом.

2

Не Парнас, не Синай,
Просто голый казарменный
Холм. – Равняйся! Стреляй! –
Отчего же глазам моим
(Раз октябрь, а не май)
Та гора была – рай?

3

Как на ладони поданный
Рай – не берись, коль жгуч!
Гора бросалась под ноги
Колдобинами круч.

Как бы титана лапами
Кустарников и хвой –
Гора хватала за полы,
Приказывала: стой!

О, далеко не азбучный
Рай – сквознякам сквозняк!
Гора валила навзничь нас,
Притягивала: ляг!

Оторопев под натиском,
– Как? Не понять и днесь! –

The mountain was – worlds!
God charges dearly for a world.

My mourning began with the mountain,
The mountain over a town.

      2

Not Parnassus, not Sinai,
Just a bare, barracks-like
Hill. – "Fall in! Aim! Fire!"
Why is it that to my eyes
(Since it was not May but October)
That mountain was paradise?

      3

As if handed to us on a platter,
Paradise! – Don't touch! It's hot!
The mountain threw itself under our feet
With all its crags and crevices.

With the Titan's paws
Of its scrub and pines –
The mountain gripped our
Coattails, demanding: Halt!

That was no textbook paradise:
A wind to end all winds!
The mountain threw us on our backs,
It pulled us to itself: Lie down!

We were dumbstruck by the onslaught.
– How? To this day, I don't know

Гора, как сводня – святости,
Указывала: здесь...

4

Персефоны зерно гранатовое,
Как забыть тебя в стужах зим?
Помню губы, двойною раковиной
Приоткрывшиеся моим.

Персефона, зерном загубленная!
Губ упорствующий багрец,
И ресницы твои – зазубринами,
И звезды золотой зубец.

5

Не обман – страсть, и не вымысел!
И не лжет, – только не дли!
О когда бы в сей мир явились мы
Простолюдинами любви!

О когда б, здраво и попросту:
Просто – холм, просто – бугор...
Говорят – тягою к пропасти
Измеряют уровень гор,

В ворохах вереска бурого,
В островах страждущих хвой...
(Высота бреда – над уровнем
Жизни)
       – На же меня! Твой...

Но семьи тихие милости,
Но птенцов лепет – увы!

The mountain – like a saintly madam,
Indicated: here.

                4

Persephone's pomegranate seed,
How to forget you in the dead of winter?
I remember lips opening up to mine
Like a seashell's matching halves.

Persephone, destroyed by a seed!
The stubborn redness of your lips,
The jagged notches of your lashes,
The golden tooth of a star…

                5

Passion is neither fraud nor fancy.
Nor does it lie – but don't drag it out!
If only we came into this world
As commoners of love!

– Simple and sensible:
This, just a hill, that, a hillock…
(They say it's by the pull of the abyss
That you measure a mountain's height.)

In the mounds of brown heather,
In the islands of tortured pines…
(The height of delirium above
The plain of life)
                    –Take me, then! I'm yours.

But the quiet rewards of family life
And the twitter of nestlings – alas, no!

Оттого что в сей мир явились мы –
Небожителями любви!

6

Гора горевала (а горы глиной
Горькой горюют в часы разлук),
Гора горевала о голубиной
Нежности наших безвестных утр.

Гора горевала о нашей дружбе:
Губ непреложнейшее родство!
Гора говорила, что коемужды
Сбудется – по *слезам* его.

Еще горевала гора, что табор –
Жизнь, что весь век по сердцам базарь!
Еще горевала гора: хотя бы
с дитятком – отпустил Агарь!

Еще говорила, что это демон
Крутит, что замысла нет в игре.
Гора говорила. Мы были немы.
Предоставляли судить горе.

7

Гора горевала, что только грустью
Станет – что ныне и кровь и зной.
Гора говорила, что не отпустит
Нас, не допустит тебя с другой!

Гора горевала, что только дымом
Станет – что ныне: и Мир, и Рим.

Because we came into this world
As divinities of love.

      6

When mountains mourn, their clay
Turns bitter in the hour of parting.
The mountain grieved for the dove-like
Tenderness of our unsung mornings.

The mountain lamented our friendship:
The absolute kinship of our lips!
The mountain said: "To each
Shall be given, according to his tears."

The mountain grieved that life is a gypsy camp
From year to year we haggle from heart to heart!
And still the mountain lamented: at least
Hagar was exiled along with her child.

And it said that a demon rolls the dice;
There's no point to the game.
The mountain spoke, and we were silent.
We left it to the mountain to judge.

      7

The mountain mourned that all will be sadness –
What is now blood and fire.
The mountain said it would not release us,
It won't let you be with someone else!

The mountain mourned that all will be smoke
What is now the World and Rome.

Гора говорила, что быть с другими
Нам (не завидую тем, другим!).

Гора горевала о страшном грузе
Клятвы, которую поздно клясть.
Гора говорила, что стар тот узел
Гордиев: долг и страсть.

Гора горевала о нашем горе:
Завтра! Не сразу! Когда над лбом
– Уж не *memento*,– а просто – *море!*
Завтра, когда поймем.

Звук... ну как будто бы кто-то просто,
Ну плачет вблизи?
Гора горевала о том, что врозь нам
Вниз, по такой грязи –

В жизнь, про которую знаем все мы:
Сброд – рынок – барак.
Еще говорила, что все поэмы
Гор – пишутся – *так.*

                 8

Та гора была, как горб
Атласа, титана стонущего.
Той горою будет горд
Город, где с утра и до ночи мы

Жизнь свою – как карту бьем!
Страстные, *не быть* упорствуем.
Наравне с медвежьим рвом
И двенадцатью апостолами –

Чтите мой угрюмый грот.
(Грот – была, и волны впрыгивали!)

The mountain said that we will be with others
(As for those others, I don't envy them!)

The mountain mourned for the terrible burden
Of an oath whose time has passed.
The mountain said that this Gordian knot
Is timeless, this one of duty and passion.

The mountain mourned for our mourning.
'Tomorrow! Not yet! When over our heads
– Hangs no longer memento, just more – the sea.
Tomorrow we shall understand.

The sound… as if someone near us…
What is it? Crying?
The mountain mourned our descent
Separately, in such mud,

Into life which we all know is just
Rabble-market-barracks…
It also said that all poems
Of mountains are written thus.

8

The mountain was like the hump
Of Atlas, that groaning Titan.
Yet it will be proud of its mountain,
This town where, from morning till night,

We trump our lives like cards!
Passionate, we insist on not being.
Just as you honour a bear's cave
And the twelve apostles –

So honour my gloomy grotto.
(I was a grotto, and the waves plunged in!)

Той игры последний ход
Помнишь – на исходе пригорода?

Та гора была – миры!
Боги мстят своим подобиям!
....
Горе началось с горы.
Та гора на мне – надгробием.

9

Минут годы. И вот – означенный
Камень, плоским смененный, снят.[1]
Нашу гору застроят дачами,
Палисадниками стеснят.

Говорят, на таких окраинах
Воздух чище и легче жить.
И пойдут лоскуты выкраивать,
Перекладинами рябить,

Перевалы мои выструнивать,
Все овраги мои – вверх дном!
Ибо надо ведь хоть кому-нибудь
Дома в счастье, и *счастья* – в дом!

Счастья – *в доме!* Любви без вымыслов!
Без вытя-гивания жил!
Надо женщиной быть – и вынести!
(Было-было, когда ходил,

Счастье – в доме!) Любви, не скрашенной
Ни разлукою, ни ножом.
На развалинах счастья нашего
Город встанет: мужей и жен.

---

[1] Т. е. вместо этого камни (горы на мне) будет плоский (плита).

Do you remember the last move
Of the game at the suburb's edge?

That mountain was – worlds!
The gods avenge their graven images!
My mourning began with the mountain,
The mountain over me is a tombstone.

9

The years will pass. And then the aforesaid rock
Will be moved, replaced by a flat one.[1]
Our mountain will be overrun with dachas,
Hemmed in by gardens.

They say that in these suburbs
The air is cleaner and life is easier.
And they will cut it into pieces,
Roofbeams will be everywhere,

They will clear away my mountain passes,
And rip up my ravines.
There has to be someone at home
With happiness, bringing happiness home.

Happiness in the home! A love without myths.
– Without the racking of veins!
One must be a woman to bear this.
(Once there was, when you would visit,

Happiness – in my home!) A love unrelieved
By parting, or the knife.
On the wreckage of our happiness
Will rise a town of husbands and wives.

---
[1] "That is, instead of this stone (the mountain on me) there'll be a flat stone (a slab).

И на том же блаженном воздухе,
– Пока можешь еще – греши! –
Будут лавочники на отдыхе
Пережевывать барыши,

Этажи и ходы надумывать,
Чтобы каждая нитка – в дом!
Ибо надо ведь хоть кому-нибудь
Крыши с аистовым гнездом!

10

Но под тяжестью тех фундаментов
Не забудет гора – игры.
Есть беспутные, нет – беспамятных:
Горы времени – у горы!

По упорствующим расселинам
Дачник, поздно хватясь, поймет:
Не пригорок, поросший семьями, –
Кратер, пущенный в оборот!

Виноградниками – Везувия
Не сковать! Великана – льном
Не связать! *Одного* безумия
Уст – достаточно, чтобы львом

Виноградники за–ворочались,
Лаву ненависти струя.
Будут девками ваши дочери
И поэтами – сыновья!

Дочь, ребенка расти внебрачного!
Сын, цыганкам себя страви!
Да не будет вам места злачного,
Телеса, на моей крови!

And in that same blessed air,
– Sin while you can! –
Shopkeepers on vacation
Will mull over their gains.

They will think up new floors and hallways,
Save every little thread – for the home.
Someone has to have
A stork's nest on the roof!

          10
But under the weight of these foundations,
The mountain will not forget the game.
Even those who are lost are not forgetful:
The mountain has mountains of time.

Seeing the obstinate crevices,
Dacha dwellers will realize, too late,
'This is no hillock overgrown with families
It's a volcano, coming to life!

A Vesuvius fettered by vineyards –
Impossible. A giant can't be bound
With flax. A single insanity
Of the lips is enough to start vineyards

Moving like lions, pouring
Out their lava of hate.
Your daughters shall be sluts,
And your sons – poets!

Daughter, bear a bastard child!
Son, let the gypsies take you away!
May you never prosper on this land,
You – bodies, feeding upon my blood.

Тверже камня краеугольного,
Клятвой смертника на одре:
Да не будет вам счастья дольнего,
Муравьи, на моей горе!

В час неведомый, в срок негаданный
Опознаете всей семьей
Непомерную и громадную
Гору заповеди седьмой!

ПОСЛЕСЛОВИЕ

Есть пробелы в памяти – бельма
На глазах: семь покрывал.
Я не помню тебя отдельно.
Вместо черт – белый провал.

Без примет. Белым пробелом –
Весь. (Душа, в ранах сплошных,
Рана – сплошь.) Частности мелом
Отмечать – дело портных.

Небосвод – цельным основан.
Океан – скопище брызг?!
Без примет. Верно – особый –
Весь. Любовь – связь, а не сыск.

Вороной, русой ли масти –
Пусть сосед скажет: он зряч.
Разве страсть – делит на части?
Часовщик я, или врач?

Ты как круг, полный и цельный:
Цельный вихрь, *полный* столбняк.
Я не помню тебя отдельно
От любви. Равенства знак.

Harder than a cornerstone, this
Curse from a death-bed:
Your happiness shall be short-lived,
You ants, on my mountain!

In an unexpected hour, unforeseen,
You will behold, you and your clan,
The enormous and immeasurable
Mountain: God's seventh command.

EPILOGUE

Gaps in memory are cataracts
On the eyes: the seven veils.
I don't remember you clearly.
A white gap instead of your face.

No distinctive marks. All of you –
A white blank. (My soul, wounded every
Where is one big wound). Let tailors
Mark the particulars with chalk.

The firmament was created whole.
And an ocean: a mass of splashes?!
No distinctive marks. You, the whole of you,
Are unique. Love is a bond, not an inquest.

Were you blond, or black-haired? Let a neighbour
Testify to that: he's not blind.
Passion has no use for detail.
What am I, a watchmaker? A doctor?

You are complete, like a circle:
Like a whole whirlwind, or: wholly stunned.
I don't remember you as separate
From love: it equals you.

(В ворохах сонного пуха:
Водопад, пены холмы –
Новизной, странной для слуха,
Вместо: я – тронное: мы...)

Но зато, в нищей и тесной
Жизни: «жизнь, как она есть» –
Я не вижу тебя совместно
Ни с одной:
           – памяти месть!

1 января – 1 февраля 1924 г.
Прага. Гора.

(In heaps of sleepy down
– Waterfalls, hills of foam –
Something new, odd to my ear,
Instead of I – a royal we…)

But in this crammed and beggarly
Life ("life as it is")
I don't see you together
With anyone else:
the revenge of memory!

1 January – 1 February 1924
Prague. The Mountain.

ПОЭМА КОНЦА

1

В небе, ржавее жести,
Перст столба.
Встал на назначенном месте,
Как судьба.

Без четверти. Исправен?
Смерть не ждет.
Преувеличенно-плавен
Шляпы взлет.

В каждой реснице – вызов.
Рот сведен.
Преувеличенно-низок
Был поклон.

– Без четверти. Точен? –
Голос лгал.
Сердце упало: что с ним?
Мозг: сигнал!

§

Небо дурных предвестий:
Ржавь и жесть.
Ждал на обычном месте.
Время: шесть.

Сей поцелуй без звука:
Губ столбняк.
Так – государыням руку,
Мертвым – так...

POEM OF THE END

1

In the sky, rustier than tin,
Is a lamppost like a finger.
He rose at the appointed place,
Like fate.

"Quarter to. Have I kept you…?"
"Death can't wait."
Exaggeratedly smooth,
The doffing of his hat.

In every eyelash, a challenge.
The mouth, contorted.
Exaggeratedly low,
His bow.

"Quarter to." "On the dot?"
His voice lied.
My heart – fell. (What's with him?)
My brain: a signal.

§

Sky of bad omens.
Rust and tin.
He waited at the usual spot.
Six o'clock.

This soundless kiss:
The stupor of the lips.
Thus – empresses' hands are kissed,
Thus – dead men's hands…

Мчащийся простолюдин
Локтем – в бок.
Преувеличенно-нуден
Взвыл гудок.

Взвыл, – как собака взвизгнул,
Длился, злясь.
(Преувеличенность жизни
В смертный час.)

То, что вчера – по пояс,
Вдруг – до звезд.
(Преувеличенно, то есть:
Во весь рост.)

Мысленно: милый, милый.
– Час? Седьмой.
В кинематограф, или?... –
Взрыв: Домой!

       2

Братство таборное, –
Вот куда вело!
Громом на голову,
Саблей наголо,

Всеми ужасами
Слов, которых ждем,
Домом рушащимся –
Слово: дом.

§

Заблудшего баловня
Вопль: домой!

A hurrying labourer
Elbows my side.
Exaggeratedly dull,
The train-whistle howled.

Howled – yelped like a dog,
On and on, angrily.
(The exaggeration of life,
In the final hour.)

What yesterday was waist-high,
Suddenly reaches the stars.
(Exaggerated, that is:
To its full height.)

Thinking: darling, darling.
"The time?" "Seven."
"To the movies, or?"
(Exclaiming) "Home!"

       2

Gypsy brotherhood –
This is where it led!
Like thunder on the head,
Or a naked blade,

All the terror
Of anticipated words,
Of a house collapsing,
That word: home.

§

A lost spoiled child
Wailing: Home!

Дитя годовалое:
«Дай» и «мой»!

Мой брат по беспутству,
Мой зноб и зной,
Так из дому рвутся,
Как ты – домой!

§

Конем, рванувшим коновязь –
Ввысь! – и веревка в прах.
Но никакого дома ведь!
Есть, – в десяти шагах:

Дом на горе. – Не выше ли?
– Дом на верху горы.
Окно под самой крышею.
– «*Не от одной зари*

Горящее?» Так сызнова
Жизнь? – Простота поэм!
Дом, это значит: из дому
В ночь.
  (О, кому повем

Печаль мою, беду мою.
Жуть, зеленее льда?...)
– Вы слишком много думали. –
Задумчивое: – Да.

   3

И – набережная. Воды
Держусь, как толщи плотной.
Семирамидины сады
Висячие – так вот вы!

A one-year-old:
"Give me! Mine!"

My brother in sin,
My fever and fervour.
They dream of running away
The way you dream of home.

§

Like a horse jerking at its tether
Up! – and the rope's in shreds.
"But we have no home!"
"Ah, but we do. Ten paces away.

The house on the mountain." "Not higher up?"
"The house at the top of the mountain,
The window under the roof."
"Burning not only with the light

Of dawn?" "So we start over again?"
"The simplicity of poems!"
Home means: out of the house
And into the night.
            (Oh, whom shall I tell

My sorrow, my grief,
Horror, greener than ice?...)
"You've been thinking too much."
Pensively: "Yes."

    3

The embankment. I keep to the water
A dense thickness.
The hanging gardens of Semiramis,
There they are!

Воды – стальная полоса
Мертвецкого оттенка –
Держусь, как нотного листка
Певица, края стенки –

Слепец ... Обратно не отдашь?
Нет? Наклонюсь – услышишь?
Всеутолительницы жажд
Держусь, как края крыши

Лунатик...
          Но не от реки
Дрожь – рождена наядой!
Реки держаться, как руки,
Когда любимый рядом –

И верен...
          Мертвые верны.
Да, но не всем в каморке...
Смерть с левой, с правой стороны –
Ты. Правый бок как мертвый.

Разительного света сноп.
Смех, как грошовый бубен.
– Нам с вами нужно бы...
                    (Озноб.)
– Мы мужественны будем'?

        4

Тумана белокурого
Волна – воланом газовым.
Надышано, накурено,
А главное – насказано!
Чем пахнет? Спешкой крайнею,
Потачкой и грешком:

The water – a steely strip of it,
Deathly pale.
I stay with it like a singer
Sticks to the score; like a blind-man

Sticks to the edge of a wall… You won't turn me back?
If I bend down, will you hear?
I stay with it, the quencher of all thirsts,
Like a sleepwalker sticks to the edge

Of a roof…
         Oh, but it's not the water
That makes me shiver – I was born a naiad.
To hold onto the river, like holding hands
When your lover's here

And faithful.
         The dead are faithful.
Yes, but not all in the same casket…
On my left side, death; on my right –
You. My right side seems dead.

A vivid sheaf of light.
Laughter, like a toy tambourine.
"We need to have a…"
                (shivering).
"Will we be brave?"

         4

A wave of blond fog
Like a gauzy flounce.
Too much breathing, too much smoking,
But mainly too much conversation!
What's that smell? The smell of haste,
Of connivance and petty sins,

Коммерческими тайнами
И бальным порошком.

Холостяки семейные
В перстнях, юнцы маститые...
Нашучено, насмеяно,
А главное – насчитано!
И крупными, и мелкими,
И рыльцем, и пушком.
... Коммерческими сделками
И бальным порошком.

(Вполоборота: *это* вот –
Наш дом? – Не я хозяйкою!)
Один – над книжкой чековой,
Другой – над ручкой лайковой,
А тот – над ножкой лаковой
Работает тишком.
...Коммерческими браками
И бальным порошком.

Серебряной зазубриной
В окне – звезда мальтийская!
Наласкано, налюблено,
А главное – натискано!
Нащипано ... (Вчерашняя
Снедь – не взыщи: с душком!)
... Коммерческими шашнями
И бальным порошком.

Цепь чересчур короткая?
Зато не сталь, а платина!
Тройными подбородками
Тряся, тельцы – телятину
Жуют. Над шейкой сахарной
Чёрт – газовым рожком.
...Коммерческими крахами
И неким порошком –

Of business secrets
And ballroom powder.

Family men who play the field,
Beringed, respectable boys…
Too much joking, too much laughing,
But mainly – too much calculation!
Big notes and small ones,
Keeping their noses clean.
…The smell of business deals
And ballroom powder.

(Aside – is this our house? I'm not mistress here!…)
One bent over his chequebook,
Another over a kid-gloved hand,
And that one working over
A cute foot in patent-leather.
…The smell of business marriages
And ballroom powder.

A silver notch in the window
The Star of Malta!
Too much stroking, too much groping
But mainly – too much squeezing.
(Yesterday's left-overs,
But who minds the smell?)
…The smell of business swindles,
And ballroom powder.

The chain's too short?
At least it's platinum, not steel!
Their triple chins shaking,
Like calves they eat their
Veal. Over a sweet neck
The devil, a gaslight.
…The smell of business failures
And of a certain powder –

Бертольда Шварца...
                    Даровит
Был – и заступник людям.
– Нам с вами нужно говорить.
Мы мужественны будем?

                5

Движение губ ловлю.
И знаю – не скажет первым.
Не любите? – Нет, люблю.
Не любите! – Но истерзан,

Но выпит, но изведен.
(Орлом озирая местность):
Помилуйте, *это* – дом?
Дом – в сердце моем. – Словесность!

Любовь, это плоть и кровь.
Цвет – собственной кровью полит.
Вы думаете, любовь –
Беседовать через столик?

Часочек – и по домам?
Как те господа и дамы?
Любовь, это значит...
                    – Храм?
Дитя, замените шрамом

На шраме! – Под взглядом слуг
И бражников? (Я, без звука:
«Любовь – это значит лук
Натянутый: лук: разлука»).

– Любовь, это значит – связь.
Всё врозь у нас: рты и жизни.

Manufactured by Bertold Schwartz,
        – a man of many gifts,
And a benefactor of mankind.
"We need to have a talk."
Will we be brave?

    5

I catch a movement of his lips,
But I know he won't say it.
"You don't love me?" "Yes, I do."
"You don't love me!" "Yes, but the misery,

I'm drained, I am at the end of my…"
(He surveys the scene like an eagle).
"You call this home?"
"My home is in my heart." "Literature!"

Love is flesh and blood, a flower
Steeped in its own blood.
Or did you think love was
A chat across a café table?

A quick hour, and then away?
Like all these gentlemen and ladies?
Love is…
      – Is it a temple?
Hardly, child; it's a scar upon

A scar. – In full view of servants
And drunks. (Soundlessly, I say,
"Love is a stretched
Bowstring: a parting shot.")

"Love is a bond."
Yet for us it is all apart: lives, lips.

(Просила ж тебя: не сглазь!
В тот час, в сокровенный, ближний,

Тот час на верху горы
И страсти. Memento – паром:
Любовь – это все дары
В костер, – и всегда – задаром!)

Рта раковинная щель
Бледна. Не усмешка – опись.
– И прежде всего одна
Постель.
       – Вы хотели пропасть

Сказать? – Барабанный бой
Перстов. – Не горами двигать!
Любовь, это значит...
            – Мой.
Я вас понимаю. Вывод?

§

Перстов барабанный бой
Растет. (Эшафот и площадь.) –
Уедем. – А я: умрем,
Надеялась. Это проще!

Достаточно дешевизн:
Рифм, рельс, номеров, вокзалов...
Любовь, это значит: жизнь.
Нет, иначе называлось

У древних...
      – Итак? –
           Лоскут.
Платка в кулаке, как рыба.
– Так едемте? – Ваш маршрут?
Яд, рельсы, свинец – на выбор!

(I begged you not to jinx it
During that blessed hour,

That hour on the heights of the mountain
That hour of passion. Memory is steam.
Love is nothing but gifts
Thrown in the fire, for nothing.)

Like a crack in a shell, his pale
Mouth. Not a smile.
"And love is, above all, a shared
Bed."
    "Or did you want to say:
Abyss?"
    The drumbeat of his
Fingers. "I can't move mountains.
Love is…"
    "Mine.
I understand you. Now what?"

§

The drumbeat of his fingers
Grows. (A scaffold and a square.)
"Let's get out of here." – I'd hoped:
"Let's die." It would be easier.

Enough cheap stuff:
Rhymes, railways, stations, hotel rooms…
"Love means: life."
"That's not what the ancients

Called it…"
    "So?"
        A scrap
Of handkerchief in a fist, fish-like.
"Shall we?" "Your way?"
Poison, rails, bullets… take your pick!

Смерть – и никаких устройств!
– Жизнь! – Как полководец римский,
Орлом озирая войск
Остаток.
   – Тогда простимся.

6

– Я этого не хотел.
Не этого, (Молча: слушай!
Хотеть – это дело тел,
А мы друг для друга – души

Отныне...) – И не сказал.
(Да, в час, когда поезд подан,
Вы женщинам, как бокал,
Печальную честь ухода

Вручаете...) – Может, бред?
Ослышался? (Лжец учтивый,
Любовнице как букет
Кровавую честь разрыва

Вручающий...) – Внятно: слог
За слогом, итак – простимся,
Сказали вы? (Как платок,
В час сладостного бесчинства

Уроненный ...) – Битвы сей
Вы – Цезарь. (О, выпад наглый!
Противнику – как трофей,
Им отданную же шпагу

Вручать!) – Продолжает. (Звон
В ушах...) – Преклоняюсь дважды:
Впервые опережен
В разрыве. – Вы это каждой?

Death – and no conditions!
– Life! – Like a Roman commander,
Surveying what's left of his
Troops.
      "Let's call it quits."

      6

This isn't what I wanted.
Not this. (Silently: listen.
Wanting is what bodies do,
Now we are only souls.)

And that's not what I said.
(The hour the train departs
You offer to women the sad honour
Of leave-taking

Like a toast.) "Are you raving? Did I
Mishear you?" (Courteous liar,
You hand your love
The bloodstained honour of parting

Like a bouquet.) Say it clearly: syllable
By syllable. "Let's call it quits,"
You said? (Like a handkerchief
Dropped in a moment of sweet

Mischief …) In this battle you are
Caesar. (What an insolent thrust:
To hand back to the opponent
The sword he surrendered

As a trophy). He continues. (A ringing
In my ears). "I have to hand it to you:
I've never before been beaten to the punch
In breaking up." "Do you say this to everyone?"

Не опровергайте! Месть,
Достойная Ловеласа.
Жест, делающий вам честь,
А мне разводящий мясо

От кости. – Смешок. Сквозь смех –
Смерть. Жест. (Никаких хотений.
Хотеть, это дело – *тех*,
А мы друг для друга – теин

Отныне ...) Последний гвоздь
Вбит. Винт, ибо гроб свинцовый.
Последнейшая из просьб.
Прошу. – Никогда ни слова

О нас ... никому из ... ну ...
Последующих. (С носилок
Так раненые – в весну!)
– О том же и вас просила б.

Колечко на память дать?
– Нет. – Взгляд, широко-разверстый,
Отсутствует. (Как печать
На сердце твое, как перстень

На руку твою ... Без сцен!
Съем.) Вкрадчивее и тише:
– Но книгу тебе? – Как всем?
Нет, вовсе их не пишите,

Книг...

§

Значит, не надо.
Значит, не надо.
Плакать не надо.

Don't deny it – a revenge
Worthy of Lovelace;
A gesture that does you credit
While it tears the flesh

From my bones. – Laughter. Beyond laughter
Death. A gesture. (No desire.
Desire is for others now,
From now on we are but shadows

For one another.) The last nail's been hammered in,
The lead coffin screwed shut.
"My last wish…"
"Of course." "Not a word

About us… to those… who
Come after me." (Thus the wounded
On their stretchers speak of spring.)
"I would ask the same of you."

"Would you like a ring for a keepsake?"
"No." "Your wide-open look
Is gone." (Like a seal on your heart,
The ring on your hand…

No scenes. I'll choke this back.)
Quietly, furtively: "How about a book?"
"Like you give all the others?
No, don't even write them,

Books…"

§

So now I mustn't
So now I mustn't
So now I mustn't cry.

В наших бродячих
Братствах рыбачьих
Пляшут – не плачут.

Пьют, а не плачут.
Кровью горячей
Платят – не плачут.

Жемчуг в стакане
Плавят – и миром
Правят – не плачут.

– Так я ухожу? – Насквозь
Гляжу. Арлекин, за верность,
Пьеретте своей – как кость
Презреннейшее из первенств

Бросающий: честь конца,
Жест занавеса. Реченье
Последнее. Дюйм свинца
В грудь: лучше бы, горячей бы

И – чище бы...
                Зубы
Втиснула в губы.
Плакать не буду.

Самую крепость –
В самую мякоть.
Только не плакать.

В братствах бродячих
Мрут, а не плачут,
Жгут, а не плачут.

В пепел и в песню
Мертвого прячут
В братствах бродячих.

In our wandering tribe's
Brotherhood, fishermen
Dance, but don't cry,

Drink, but don't cry.
With their hot blood
They pay, but don't cry.

They melt pearls
In a glass and rule their world
But don't cry.

"So I leave first?" I can see through
Him. Harlequin hands to his faithful
Pierrette the most paltry victory,
Like a bone:

The honour of the ending,
Of bringing down the curtain. The last
Word. An inch of lead in the breast
Would be better, and hotter,

And cleaner...
               Teeth
Biting lips. I
Won't cry.

The sharpest –
Against the softest.
Only no crying.

In the wandering brotherhoods
They die but don't cry,
Burn, but don't cry.

They hide the dead
In ashes and song
In the wandering brotherhoods.

– Так первая? Первый ход?
Как в шахматы, значит? Впрочем,
Ведь даже на эшафот
Нас первыми просят...
                      – Срочно
Прошу, не глядите! – Взгляд. –
(Вот-вот уже хлынут градом!
Ну как их загнать назад
В глаза?!) – Говорю, не надо

Глядеть!!!

Внятно и громко,
Взгляд в вышину:
– Милый, уйдемте,
Плакать начну!

§

Забыла! Среди копилок
Живых (коммерсантов – тож!)
Белокурый сверкнул затылок:
Маис, кукуруза, рожь!

Все заповеди Синая
Смывая – менады мех! –
Голконда волосяная,
Сокровищница утех –

(Для всех!) Не напрасно копит
Природа, не сплошь скупа!
Из сих белокурых тропик,
Охотники, – где тропа

Назад? Наготою грубой
Дразня и слепя до слез –
Сплошным золотым прелюбом
Смеющимся пролилось.

"So I go first? I make the first move?
As in chess? We get to be first
Even on the scaffold…
                        This is urgent;

I beg you, don't look." He looks.
(Another second and they'll fall.
How can I chase them back into
My eyes? "I'm telling you, don't

Look!!!"

Loud and clear,
My eyes toward the sky:
"Darling, let's go,
Or else I'll cry!"

§

I forgot! Among the walking
Strongboxes (entrepreneurs!)
A blond head of hair:
Maize, corn, rye.

Washing away all the commandments
Of Sinai – Mænad's fur! –
A horsehair Golcond,
A treasury of delights

(For all). Nature hoards, not in vain;
She's not always miserly.
Hunters, show me the way,
Out of these fair-headed

Tropics. Teasing with crude
Nudity, blinding me to tears.
Sheer golden laughing
Lust poured down.

– Не правда ли? – Льнущий, мнущий
Взгляд. В каждой реснице – эуд.
– И главное – эта гуща!
Жест, скручивающий в жгут.

О, рвущий уже одежды –
Жест! Проще, чем пить и есть –
Усмешка! (Тебе надежда,
Увы, на спасенье есть!)

И – сестрински или братски?
Союзнически: союз!
– Не похоронив – смеяться!
(И похоронив – смеюсь.)

7

И – набережная. Последняя.
Все. Порознь и без руки,
Чурающимися соседями
Бредем. Со стороны реки –

Плач. Падающую соленую
Ртуть слизываю без забот:
Луны огромной Соломоновой
Слезам не выслал небосвод.

Столб. Отчего бы лбом не стукнуться
В кровь? Вдребезги бы, а не в кровь!
Страшащимися сопреступниками
Бредем. (Убитое – Любовь.)

Брось! Разве это двое любящих?
В ночь? Порознь? С другими спать?
– Вы понимаете, что будущее –
Там? – Запрокидываюсь вспять.

"Isn't it so?" A clinging, crumpling
Look. In each of his lashes a sensual itch.
And especially their thickness!
A plait-twisting gesture.

A gesture that strips away clothes –
It's simpler than eating or drinking.
He grins. (Alas, you can still
Count on being saved.)

Sisterly or brotherly?
Anyway, a bond.
"Laughter at a funeral!"
(Even when it's over, I laugh.)

      7

And the embankment. The last one.
It's all over. Apart, hands not touching,
We walk like neighbours shunning
One another. From the riverside –

Tears. Carelessly I lick off
Salty quicksilver falling on my lips.
The heavens didn't send out a great
Moon of Solomon for my tears.

A lamppost. Why not beat my forehead
Bloody against it? To smithereens!
We walk like frightened partners
In crime. (The victim was love.)

Really! These two are lovers?
Going separately – into the night – to sleep with others?
"You understand that the future is
There?" I toss back my head.

Спать! – Новобрачными по коврику...
Спать! – Все не попадаем в шаг,
В такт. Жалобно: – Возьмите под руку!
Не каторжники, чтобы так!...

Ток. (Точно мне *душою* – на руку
Лег! – На руку рукою.) Ток
Бьет, проводами лихорадочными
Рвет, – на душу рукою лег!

Льнет. Радужное все! Что радужнее
Слез? Занавесом, чаще бус,
Дождь. – Я таких не знаю набережных
Кончающихся. – Мост, и:
                    – Ну-с?

Здесь? (Дроги поданы).
Спо-койных глаз
Взлет. – Можно до дому?
В по-следний раз!

           8

По-следний мост.
(Руки не отдам, не выну!)
Последний мост,
Последняя мостовина.

Во – да и твердь.
Выкладываю монеты.
День – га за смерть,
Харонова мзда за Лету.

Мо-неты тень
В руке теневой. Без звука
Мо-неты те.
Итак, в теневую руку –

To sleep! – Like newlyweds stepping over their carpet…
To sleep! – We still can't fall into step,
Into rhythm. I beg miserably: take my arm,
We don't have to walk like convicts.

A shock. (As if his soul leaned on
My arm. His arm on mine.) The current
Flows, feverish wires rip,
Tear. He's leaned on my soul with his arm.

He clings. Everything's a rainbow! What's more
Like a rainbow than tears? A curtain denser than beads,
The rain falls. "I don't know if such embankments
End." "A bridge, and
                      Well then?

Here?" (The hearse is waiting.)
His calm eyes move
Upwards. "Will you see me home?"
For the last time.

      8

The last bridge.
(I won't release my hand, or withdraw it!)
The last bridge,
The last toll.

Water, and solid ground.
I take out coins
Death's toll,
Charon's price for Lethe.

The shadow of money
In a shadow hand. Soundless,
These coins. So,
Into the shade's hand

Мо-неты тень.
Без отсвета и без звяка.
Мо-неты – тем.
С умерших довольно маков.

Мост.

§

Бла-гая часть
Любовников без надежды:
Мост, ты – как страсть:
Условность: сплошное между.

Гнезжусь: тепло,
Ребро – потому и льну так.
Ни *до,* ни *по:*
Прозрения промежуток!

Ни рук, ни ног.
Всей костью и всем упором:
Жив только бок,
О смежный теснюсь которым.

Вся жизнь – в боку!
Он – ухо и он же – эхо.
Желтком к белку
Леплюсь, самоедом к меху

Теснюсь, леплюсь,
Мощусь. Близнецы Сиама,
Что – ваш союз?
Та женщина – помнишь: мамой

Звал? всё и вся
Забыв, в торжестве недвижном
Те-бя нося,
Тебя не держала ближе.

I place the shadow of the coin
Without clink or glitter.
This coin's for them.
Poppies will do for the dead.

The bridge.

§

The happy lot
Of lovers without hope:
Bridge, you are like passion:
A convention: pure transition.

I nestle. It's warm,
Adam's rib – that's why I cling.
Neither before, nor after:
An interval of insight.

No arms, no legs.
All bone and pushing.
Only my side is alive,
Pressing against you.

All my life's in that side!
It's an ear and an echo.
I stick to you like the yolk to the white,
Like a Samoyed to his fur.

I cling, I cleave to you.
The bond of Siamese twins,
What's it to ours?
That woman, remember,

You called Mother – oblivious to all
In her motionless triumph,
Carrying you,
Even she never held you closer.

Пойми! Сжились!
Сбылись! На груди баюкал!
Не – брошусь вниз!
Нырять – отпускать бы руку

При–шлось. И жмусь,
И жмусь... И неотторжима.
Мост, ты не муж:
Любовник – сплошное мимо!

Мост, ты за нас!
Мы реку телами кормим!
Плю–щом впилась,
Клещом: вырывайте с корнем!

Как плющ! как клещ!
Безбожно! Бесчеловечно!
Бро–сать, как вещь,
Меня, ни единой вещи

Не чтившей в сём
Вещественном мире дутом!
Скажи, что сон!
Что ночь, а за ночью – утро,

Эк–спресс и Рим!
Гренада? Сама не знаю,
Смахнув перин
Монбланы и Гималаи.

Про–гал глубок:
Последнею кровью грею.
Про–слушай бок!
Ведь это куда вернее

Сти–хов... Прогрет
Ведь? Завтра к кому наймешься?

Understand: we've merged!
You cradled me on your chest.
I can't jump off now,
Diving now would mean letting go

Of your hand. I press and press
Against you…. I can't be torn away.
Bridge, you're no husband,
You're a lover: a pure transition.

Bridge, you're on our side:
We feed the river with our bodies.
I bite you like a tick, I'm like ivy:
Tear me out by the roots!

Like ivy! Like a tick!
Godless! Inhuman!
To throw me out like a thing,
Me, who never valued a thing

In all this fake,
Thing-laden world!
Tell me I'm dreaming!
That it's night, and after the night is morning,

An express, and Rome!
Or Granada? I won't know
Throwing off the Mont Blancs and Himalayas
Of bedclothes.

This gash is deep.
I warm it with my last blood.
Feel my side:
It is far truer

Than poems. Warmed through,
Aren't you? Who will you pay tomorrow

Ска—жи, что бред!
Что нет и не будет мосту

Кон—ца...
        – Конец.

§

– Здесь? – Детский, божеский
Жест. – Ну-с? – Впилась. –
Е—ще немножечко:
В последний раз!

9

Корпусами фабричными, зычными
И отзывчивыми на зов...
Сокровенную, подъязычную
Тайну жен от мужей, и вдов

От друзей – тебе, подноготную
Тайну Евы от древа – вот:
Я не более чем животное,
Кем-то раненное в живот.

Жжет... Как будто бы душу сдернули
С кожей! Паром в дыру ушла
Пресловутая ересь вздорная,
Именуемая душа.

Христианская немочь бледная!
Пар! Припарками обложить!
Да ее никогда и не было!
Было тело, хотело жить,

Жить не хочет.

For warmth? Tell me this is delirium.
That this bridge has no

End. Will never —
                    The end.

§

"Here?" A childlike, godlike
Gesture. "Well?" I cling.
"A little bit farther.
For the last time!"

                    9

Like factory buildings, loud
And responsive to your call,
Here's the innermost, visceral
Secret that wives keep from husbands,

Widows from friends; here is
The cherished secret Eve took from the tree:
I'm no better than a beast
Wounded in the gut.

It burns… As if my soul were torn
Away with the skin. Like steam through a hole,
It vanished, that notorious silly heresy
Called the soul.

That Christian anaemia!
Steam! (Cover it with a poultice!)
There never was any such thing!
Only a body which wanted to live,

And no longer wants to.

§

Прости меня! Не хотела!
Вопль вспоротого нутра!
Так смертники ждут расстрела
В четвертом часу утра

За шахматами... Усмешкой
Дразня коридорный глаз.
Ведь шахматные же пешки!
И кто-то играет в нас.

Кто? Боги благие? Воры?
Во весь окоем глазка –
Глаз. Красного коридора
Лязг. Вскинутая доска.

Махорочная затяжка.
Сплёв, пожили значит, сплёв
...По сим тротуарам в шашку
Прямая дорога: в ров

И в кровь. Потайное око:
Луны слуховой глазок...
....
И покосившись сбоку:
– Как ты уже далек!

10

Совместный и сплоченный
Вздрог. – Наша молочная!

Наш остров, наш храм,
Где мы по утрам –

§

Forgive me! I didn't mean it!...
The howl of ripped entrails!
Thus at four in the morning
The condemned wait to be shot,

Playing chess, with a grin
Teasing the corridor's eye.
We're pawns in a chess game,
And someone's playing with us.

Who? Kind gods? Or thieves?
Filling the entire keyhole –
An eye. Along the red corridor
A clank. The bolt shoots back.

A drag on a cigarette.
(Spit.) We did some living. (Spit.)
Along this chequered pavement is
The road straight to the pit.

To blood. A secret eye:
The dormer eye of the moon…
……………………………………
And looking at you sideways:
"How far away you already are!"

      10

A shared, simultaneous
Shudder: There's our coffee shop!

Our island, our shrine,
Where in the morning we –

Сброд! Пара минутная! –
Справляли заутреню.

Базаром и закисью,
Сквозь-сном и весной...
Здесь кофе был пакостный, –
Совсем овсяной!

(Овсом своенравие
Гасить в рысаках!)
Отнюдь не Аравией –
Аркадией пах

Тот кофе...

Но как улыбалась нам,
Рядком усадив,
Бывалой и жалостной, –
Любовниц седых

Улыбкою бережной:
Увянешь! Живи!
Безумью, безденежью,
Зевку и любви, –

А главное – юности!
Смешку – без причин,
Усмешке – без умысла,
Лицу – без морщин, –

О, главное – юности!
Страстям не по климату!
Откуда-то дунувшей,
Откуда-то хлынувшей

В молочную тусклую:
– Бурнус и Тунис! –

Rabble! A chance couple!
Conducted our matins.

A smell of market stalls and sourness,
Of drowsiness and spring…
The coffee was lousy –
Really nothing but oats in it.

(Oats to extinguish,
The racehorses' wildness.)
Not of Arabia,
But of Arcadia

The coffee's smell…

But how she smiled at us,
Sitting us down,
Worldly-wise, sorrowful,
With a grey-haired lover's

Solicitous smile:
You'll wither! Live now!
A smile at our penniless madness,
Our yawns and love,

But mainly at youth,
At laughter without cause,
At smiles without thought,
Faces without creases.

Oh, mainly at youth!
At passions out of climate,
Blown in from somewhere
Flown in from somewhere

Into the dim coffee shop –
Burnoose and Tunis,

Надеждам и мускулам
Под ветхостью риз...

(Дружочек, не жалуюсь:
Рубец на рубце!)
О, как провожала нас
Хозяйка в чепце

Голландского глаженья...

§

Не довспомнивши, не допонявши,
Точно с праздника уведены...
Наша улица! – Уже не наша... –
Сколько раз по ней... – Уже не мы... –

– Завтра с западу встанет солнце!
– С Иеговой порвет Давид!
– Что мы делаем? – Расстаемся.
– Ничего мне не говорит

Сверхбессмысленнейшее слово:
Рас–стаемся. – Одна из ста?
Просто слово в четыре слога,
За которыми пустота.

Стой! По-сербски и по-кроатски,
Верно, Чехия в нас чудит?
Рас–ставание. Расставаться...
Сверхъестественнейшая дичь!

Звук, от коего уши рвутся,
Тянутся за предел тоски...
Расставание – не по-русски!
Не по-женски! не по-мужски!

At hopes and muscles
Under worn-out clothes.

(My friend, I'm not complaining.
Scars upon scars.
Oh, how she saw us off,
Our hostess in her cap,

Stiff as Dutch linen.

§

Half-remembered; half-grasped,
As if taken too soon from a party…
"Our street!" "No longer ours…"
"How many times we…" "No longer will we…"

"Tomorrow the sun will rise in the West!"
"David will break with Jehovah!"
"What are we doing? "Separating."
"That word means nothing to me."

The most meaningless word:
Separating. Am I one of a hundred?
Just four syllables
After which comes emptiness.

Wait! Is it Serbian or Croatian?
Maybe Czech is playing us false?
Separation. Separating…
The most preternatural nonsense.

A howl that rips the ears,
Stretched out beyond the bounds of pain.
Separation – it's not Russian talk.
Not women's, nor men's.

Не по-божески! Что мы – овцы,
Раззевавшиеся в обед?
Расставание – по-каковски?
Даже смысла такого нет,

Даже звука! Ну, просто полый
Шум – пилы, например, сквозь сон.
Расставание – просто школы
Хлебникова соловьиный стон,

Лебединый...
          Но как же вышло?
Точно высохший водоем –
Воздух! Руку о руку слышно.
Расставаться – ведь это гром

На голову... Океан в каюту!
Океании крайний мыс!
Эти улицы – слишком круты:
Расставаться – ведь это вниз,

Под гору... Двух подошв пудовых
Вздох... Ладонь, наконец, и гвоздь!
Опрокидывающий довод:
Расставаться – ведь это врозь,

Мы же – сросшиеся...

11

Разом проигрывать –
Чище нет!
Загород, пригород:
Дням конец.

Негам (читай – камням),
Дням, и домам, и нам.

Nor God's. What are we, sheep,
Gaping at our dinner?
Separation – in what language?
There's no sense in it,

No sound. Just a hollow noise
Like a handsaw heard, say, through sleep.
Separation: it's like Khlebnikov's
Nightingale moans,

Swanlike…
        But how did it happen?
Like a dried-out river bed –
The air! A handclap can be heard.
Separation is a clap of thunder

Over our heads. The ocean flooding the cabin.
Oceania's farthest cape!
These streets are too steep.
Separation is descent –

Down the mountain… the sigh of two massive
Shoes. At last, the palm, and the nail in it.
This overpowering argument:
Separation means we must part,

We, who had grown to be as one.

11

Losing everything at once –
There's nothing neater.
Suburbs, outskirts:
End to our days.

End to our joys (read "burdens"),
The days, houses, and us.

Дачи пустующие! Как мать
Старую – так же чту их.
Это ведь действие – пустовать:
Полое не пустует.

(Дачи, пустующие на треть,
Лучше бы вам сгореть!)

Только не вздрагивать,
Рану вскрыв.
Загород, загород,
Швам разрыв!

Ибо – без лишних слов
Пышных – любовь есть шов.

Шов, а не перевязь, шов – не щит.
– О, не проси защиты! –
Шов, коим мертвый к земле пришит,
Коим к тебе пришита.

(Время покажет еще, каким:
Легким или тройным!)

Так или иначе, друг, – по швам!
Дребезги и осколки!
Только и славы, что треснул сам:
Треснул, а не расползся!

Что под наметкой – живая жиль
Красная, а не гниль!

О, не проигрывает –
Кто рвет!
Загород, пригород:
Лбам развод.

Empty dachas: I revere them
As I would an aged mother.
This is an action, after all, – to vacate:
What's empty can't be emptied.

(Dachas, one-third empty,
You'd do better to burn!)

Just don't wince,
When the wound is open.
To the outskirts, way out of town,
To rip out the stitches.

For, to say it plainly, simply:
Love is a seam.

A seam, not a sling; a stitch, not a shield.
Oh, don't ask to be shielded!
The stitch by which the dead are sewn to the earth,
By which I'm stitched to you.

(Time will prove what kind of seam:
Single or reinforced.)

Either way, friend, rip out the stitches!
Shreds and Fragments!
It's good it ripped by itself –
Better to rip than unravel.

And under the basting – a live red
Vein, and not decay.

Oh, he who rips and tears
Knows no loss!
To the outskirts, way out of town:
Foreheads' divorce.

По слободам казнят
Нынче, – мозгам сквозняк!

О, не проигрывает, кто прочь –
В час, как заря займется.
Целую жизнь тебе сшила в ночь
Набело, без наметки.

Так не кори же меня, что вкривь.
Пригород: швам разрыв.

Души неприбранные –
В рубцах!...
Загород, пригород...
Яр размах

Пригорода. Сапогом судьбы,
Слышишь – по глине жидкой?
...Скорую руку мою суди,
Друг, да живую нитку

Цепкую – как ее ни канай!
По–следний фонарь!

§

Здесь? Словно заговор –
Взгляд. Низших рас –
Взгляд. – Можно на гору?
В по–следний раз!

12

Частой гривою
Дождь в глаза. – Холмы.
Миновали пригород.
За городом мы.

A draft in the brain:
An execution on the outskirts today.

Oh, he who leaves knows no loss
When the dawn is breaking.
I have sewn your entire life in one night,
Perfectly, without basting.

So don't reproach me if it's crooked.
Outskirts: ripping out the stitches.

Untidy souls,
Covered with welts!…
To the outskirts, way out of town…
Violent the sweep

Of the suburbs. Fate's heel
On the wet clay – you hear it?
…Blame my hurried hand,
My friend, and the live clinging

Thread – however tangled.
The last street lamp.

§

Here? Like in a conspiracy –
A look. From an inferior race –
A look. Can we climb the mountain?
For the last time.

12

Like a thick mane,
The rain in our eyes. – Hills.
We've passed the outskirts.
We're far out of town.

Есть – да нету нам!
Мачеха – не мать!
Дальше некуда.
Здесь околевать.

Поле. Изгородь.
Брат стоим с сестрой.
Жизнь есть пригород. –
За городом строй!

Эх, проигранное
Дело, господа!
Все-то – пригороды!
Где же города?!

Рвет и бесится
Дождь. Стоим и рвем.
За три месяца
Первое вдвоем!

И у Иова,
Бог, хотел взаймы?
Да не выгорело:
За городом мы!

§

За городом! Понимаешь? Зá!
Вне! Перешед вал!
Жизнь – это место, где жить нельзя:
Ев-рейский квартал...

Так не достойнее ль во сто крат
Стать Вечным Жидом?
Ибо для каждого, кто не гад,
Ев-рейский погром –

It's there, but not for us!
A stepmother, not a mother!
Nowhere further.
Here's where we croak.

A field. A fence.
We're brother and sister.
Life is an exurb:
Build it way out of town.

Ahh, the game's lost,
Ladies and gentlemen!
Suburbs everywhere!
Where are the real cities?

Rain rips and rages.
We stand, and rip.
In three months, this is
Our first time together!

God, you wanted
A loan, even from Job?
But that didn't work:
We're way out of town.

§

Out of town! You understand? Outside!
Out! We've breached the walls.
Life is a place where no one can live:
The Jewish quarter…

Wouldn't it be a hundred times better
To become the Wandering Jew?
For anyone not scum,
Life is a pogrom.

Жизнь. Только выкрестами жива!
Иудами вер!
На прокаженные острова!
В ад! – всюду! – но не в

Жизнь, – только выкрестов терпит, лишь
Овец – палачу!
Право-на-жительственный свой лист
Но–гами топчу!

Втаптываю! За Давидов щит –
Месть! – В месиво тел!
Не упоительно ли, *что* жид
Жить – не захотел?!

Гетто избранничеств! Вал и ров.
По–щады не жди!
В сем христианнейшем нз миров
Поэты – жиды!

13

Так ножи вострят о камень,
Так опилки метлами
Смахивают. Под руками
Меховое, мокрое.

Где ж вы, двойни:
Сушь мужская, мощь?
Под ладонью –
Слезы, а не дождь!

О каких еще соблазнах –
Речь? Водой – имущество!
После глаз твоих алмазных,
Под ладонью льющихся, –

Life loves only converts,
Judases of all faiths!
Go to a leper colony! To hell!
Anywhere, but not into life,

It spares only traitors,
Sheep for the butcher!
My birth certificate
I trample underfoot!

I trample it! Vengeance:
David's shield revenged. Into the crush of bodies.
Isn't it thrilling that the yid
Did not want to live?

The ghetto of the chosen few. The wall and the ditch.
Expect no mercy.
In this most Christian of worlds
All poets are yids.

13

Thus they sharpen knives on stone,
Thus they sweep the shavings out
With brooms. Under my hands –
Something wet and furry.

Where are you, you twins:
Masculine dryness, strength?
Under my palm,
Tears, not rain.

What greater temptations
To speak of? My wealth is in water.
Since I felt your diamond eyes
Begin to flow under my palm,

Нет пропажи
Мне. Конец концу!
Глажу – глажу –
Глажу по лицу.

Такова у нас, Маринок,
Спесь, – у нас, полячек-то.
После глаз твоих орлиных,
Под ладонью плачущих...

Плачешь? Друг мой!
Все мое! Прости!
О, как крупно,
Солоно в горсти!

Жестока слеза мужская:
Обухом по темени!
Плачь, с другими наверстаешь
Стыд, со мной потерянный.

Оди−накового
Моря – рыбы! Взмах:
...Мертвой раковиной
Губы на губах,

В слезах.
Лебеда –
На вкус.
– А завтра,
Когда
Проснусь?

14

Тропою овечьей –
Спуск. Города гам.

Nothing's lost to me.
An end to the ending.
I stroke – and stroke –
And stroke your face.

That's the sort of pride we have,
We Marinas, we Polish girls.
After your eagle's eyes
Wept under my palm…

Crying? My friend, my
Everything! Forgive me.
How large and salty
They feel in my hand.

Men's tears are cruel:
Like a crack on the head.
Weep! With others you'll recover
The dignity you lost with me.

We are fish of one
Sea. An upward sweep!
…Like a dead seashell,
Lips upon lips.

In tears.
Bitter taste
Of goosefoot.
And tomorrow,
When
I wake?

14

The descent like a sheep-
Path. City noise.

Три девки навстречу.
Смеются. Слезам

Смеются, – всем полднем
Недр, гребнем морским!
Смеются!
           – недолжным,
Позорным, мужским

Слезам твоим, видным
Сквозь дождь – в два рубца!
Как жемчуг – постыдным
На бронзе бойца.

Слезам твоим первым,
Последним, – о, лей! –
Слезам твоим – перлам
В короне моей!

Глаз явно не туплю.
Сквозь ливень – перюсь.
Венерины куклы,
Вверяйтесь! Союз

Сей более тесен,
Чем влечься и лечь.
Самой Песней Песен
Уступлена речь

Нам, птицам безвестным
Челом Соломон
Бьет, – ибо совместный
Плач – больше, чем сон!

§

Three tarts come towards us.
Laughing. At your tears.

They laugh, their wombs like ripe noon,
 Their swelling crests of waves,
They laugh at your unseemly,
Disgraceful, male –

At your tears, visible
Through the rain like welts;
Like pearls, shameful
On a warrior's bronze.

At your first and last
Tears – Let them flow!
At your tears, the pearls
In my crown!

I won't lower my eyes.
I stare through the downpour.
Stare, puppets of Venus,
Stare! This bond

Is closer than
Luring and laying.
Even the Song of Songs
Yields to our speech.

To us, obscure little birds,
Even Solomon bows,
For our weeping together
Surpasses a dream.

§

И в полые волны
Мглы – сгорблен и равн –
Бесследно – безмолвно –
Как тонет корабль.

Прага, 1 февраля – Иловищи, 8 июня 1924 г.

So, into the hollow waves
Of darkness – hunched over
Without a sound, without a trace,
As a ship sinks.

Prague, 1 February 1924 – Ilovišči, 8 June 1924

ПОПЫТКА КОМНАТЫ

Стены косности сочтены
До меня. Но – заскок? случайность? –
Я запомнила три стены.
За четвертую не ручаюсь.

Кто же знает, спиной к стене?
Может *быть*, но ведь может *не*

Быть. И не было. Дуло. Но
Не стена за спиной – так...? Всё, что
Не угодно. Депеша «Дно»,
Царь отрекся. Не только с почты

Вести. Срочные провода
Отовсюду и отвсегда.

На рояле играл? Сквозит.
Дует. Парусом ходит. Ватой –
Пальцы. Лист сонатинный взвит.
(Не забудь, что тебе – девятый).

Для невиданной той стены
Знаю имя: стена спины

За роялем. Еще – столом
Письменным, а еще – прибором
Бритвенным (у стены – прием –
Этой – делаться коридором

В зеркале. *Перенес* – взглянул.
Пустоты переносный стул).

ATTEMPT AT A ROOM

Walls of torpor have been numbered
Before. But – a slip? A twist of fate? –
I remember three walls,
I can't vouch for the fourth.

Who can tell, with their back to the wall?
Maybe it was there, maybe

Not. It wasn't. A draft, then. Yet
If not a wall behind me – what?
Whatever's not wished for. A dispatch, Dno,
And the Tsar's abdication. News arriving

Not only by mail. Urgent wires
From everywhere and every when.

Were you playing the piano? A breeze.
A draft. Luffing like a sail. Cottony
Fingers. A sonata page flutters.
(Don't forget: the ninth is yours.)

For that unseen wall,
I have a name: the wall of a back

Bent over a piano, a desk,
Or even a shaving kit.
(This wall has a way of
Becoming a corridor

In the mirror. You glance – it's there.
A portable chair of emptiness.)

Стул для всех, кому не войти —
Дверью, — чуток порог к подошвам!
Та стена, из которой *ты*
Вырос — поторопилась с прошлым —

Между нами еще абзац
Целый. Вырастешь как Данзас —

Сзади.
      Ибо Данзасом — *та*,
Званым, избранным, с часом, с весом,
(Знаю имя: стена хребта!)
Входит в комнату — не Дантесом.

Оборот головы. — Готов?
Так и ты через десять строф,

Строк.
      Глазная атака в тыл.
Но, оставив разряд заспинный,
Потолок достоверно — *был,*
Не упорствую: как в гостиной,

Может быть и чуть-чуть косил.
(Штыковая атака в тыл —
Сил).

      И вот уже мозжечка
Сжим. Как глыба спина расселась.
Та сплошная стена Чека,
Та — рассветов, ну та — расстрелов

Светлых: четче, чем на тени
Жестов — в спину из-за спины.

То, чего не пойму: расстрел.
Но, оставив разряд застенный,

A chair for all who can't come in
The door – the threshold is sensitive to shoe soles!
That wall out of which you
Emerged – it rushed to bring in the past –

Between us, there's still an entire
Paragraph. You'll appear like Danzas –

From behind it.
Because it, like Danzas,
Invited and chosen, bringing the hour and the day,
(I know its name: the wall of a back!)
Enters the room not as D'Anthès would.

A turn of the head. – Ready?
As you will, in ten stanzas,

Or lines.
        A staring attack, on the rearguard.
But leaving aside the behind-the-back theme,
The ceiling definitely was there,
Though I won't insist it was like a parlour's,

Maybe it was even a bit awry.
(A bayonet charge
Into the rearguard.)

        Here already the squeeze of
Cerebellum. The back slumped in a mound.
The sheer wall of the Cheka,
A wall of dawns, of sunlit firing

Squads, of gestures more clear-cut than
In the shade – shot from behind, in the back.

What I can't understand: executions.
But, leaving aside the torture-chamber theme,

Потолок достоверно цел
Был (еще впереди – зачем нам

Он). К четвертой стене вернусь:
Та, куда, отступая, трус
Оступается.

      «Ну, а пол –
Был? На чем-нибудь да ведь надо ж?...»
Был. – Не всем. – На качель, на ствол,
На коня, на канат, на шабаш, –

Выше!...
      Всем нам на *«тем свету»*
С пустотою сращать пяту
Тяготенную.

      Пол – для ног.
– Как внедрен человек, как вкраплен! –
Чтоб не капало – потолок.
Помнишь, старая казнь – по капле

В час? Трава не росла бы в дом –
Пол, земля не вошла бы в дом –

Всеми – теми – кому и кол
Не препятствие ночью майской!
Три стены, потолок и пол.
Всё, как будто? Теперь – являйся!

Оповестит ли ставнею?
Комната наспех составлена,
Белесоватым по серу –
В черновике набросана.

Не штукатур, не кровельщик –
Сон. На путях беспроволочных

The ceiling was definitely
Intact. (That's still ahead of us – of what

Use is it now?) I will return to the fourth wall
At which, retreating, a coward
Halts.

      "And a floor – eh?
You must've… on something…"
Yes, though not everyone needs it
On the swings, on a tree trunk,
On a horse, a tightrope, on a binge, –

And even higher! …
                All of us, in that other world,
Will learn to walk upon
Emptiness.

A floor is for feet…
How embedded man is, how rooted!
So it won't leak: a ceiling.
Remember the ancient torture, one drop

Per hour? A floor: so that grass won't
Grow into the house, so earth won't enter –

For all those for whom even a fence
Is no obstacle on a May night!
Three walls, a ceiling, and a floor.
All set? Now, materialize!

Will the shutters announce his coming?
The room is put together slapdash,
Jotted down on a scratch pad
Whitish on grey.

Not by a plasterer, nor a roofer
But a dream, a guard on wireless

Страж. В пропастях под веками
Некий нашедший некую.

Не поставщик, не мебельщик –
Сон, поголее ревельской
Отмели. Пол без блёсткости.
Комната? Просто – плоскости.

Дебаркадер приветливей!
Нечто из геометрии,
Бездны в картонном томике,
Поздно, но полно, понятой.

А фаэтонов тормоз-то –
Стол? Да ведь локтем кормится
Стол. Разлоктись по склонности,
Будет и стол – настольности.

Так же, как деток – аисты:
Будет нужда – и явится
Вещь. Не пекись за три версты!
Стул вместе с гостем вырастет.

Все вырастет,
Не ладь, не строй.
Под вывеской
Сказать – какой?

Взаимности
Лесная глушь
Гостиница
Свиданье Душ.

Дом встречи. Все – разлуки –
Те, хоть южны́м на юг!
Прислуживают – руки?
Нет, то, что тише рук,

Pathways; a He meeting a She
In chasms underneath eyelids.

Not a supplier, nor a furniture maker –
A dream, even barer than the
Shallows at Revel. The unsparkling
Floor. A room? Mere surfaces.

Even platforms are friendlier!
Something from geometry,
That abyss in a cardboard volume
Understood too late, though fully.

And is that table the phaeton's
Brake? After all, the desk is fed by
An elbow. Elbow out along its inclines –
That will be your desk's deskness.

Just like storks carrying babies –
When you need the thing,
It will be there. Don't fret beforehand.
The chair will arise with the guest.

It will all grow well,
Don't plot and plan
At the signboard of…
(Should I tell?…)

Reciprocity's
Backwoods
Inn:
The Rendezvous of Souls.

A meeting-house. All partings
Off to the south, with the south wind.
Are those hands, serving us?
No, something quieter than hands,

И легче рук, и чище
Рук. Подновленный хлам
С услугами? Тощища
Оставленная там!

Да, здесь мы недотроги,
И в праве. Рук — гонцы,
Рук — мысли, рук — итоги,
Рук — самые концы...

Без судорожных «где ж ты?».
Жду. С тишиной в родстве,
Прислуживают — жесты
В Психеином дворце.

Только ветер поэту дорог!
В чем уверена — в коридорах.

Прохожденье — вот армий база.
Должно долго идти, чтоб сразу

Середь комнаты, с видом бога —
Лиродержца...
          — Стиха дорога!

Ветер, ветер, над лбом — как стягом
Подымаемый нашим шагом!

Водворенное «и так дале» —
Коридоры: домашнесть дали.

С грачьим профилем иноверки
Тихой скоростью даль, по мерке

Детских ног, в дождеватом пруфе
Рифмы милые: грифель — туфель —

And lighter than hands, and cleaner
Than hands. Patched up junk,
And service? – That monotony's
Left behind!

Here we're touch-me-nots
And rightly so: hands' messengers,
Hands' thoughts, hands' outcomes,
Hands' outermost limits.

Without feverish "where-are-yous?"
I wait. Akin to silence,
Gestures serve me
In Psyche's hall.

Only wind is prized by the poet!
What I'm sure of are the corridors.

Passing through – that's the army's base.
Have to march for a long time,

So as to stand in the middle of the room
Like the god of the lyre…
                     – That's the poem's path!

Wind, wind, over the forehead, like a pennant
Raised by our tread!

Settled "and-so-forth" in the
 Corridors: the distant made homey.

With a heretic's rook-like profile,
With silent speed, distance the size

Of children's feet, in rain-proof
Sweet rhymes: grifel – tufel –

Кафель ... в павлиноватом шлейфе
Где-то башня, зовется Эйфель.

Как река для ребенка – галька,
Дали – долька, не даль – а далька,

В детской памяти, струнной, донной –
Даль с ручным багажом, даль – бонной...

Не сболтнувшая нам (даль в модах)
Что там тащится на подводах...

Доведенная до пенала...
Коридоры: домов каналы.

Свадьбы, судьбы, событья, сроки, –
Коридоры: домов притоки.

В пять утра, с письмецом подметным,
Коридором не только метлы

Ходят. Тмином разит и дерном.
Род занятия? Ко–ри–дорный.

То лишь требуя, что смолола –
Коридорами – Карманьола!

Кто коридоры строил
(Рыл), знал куда загнуть,
Чтобы дать время крови
За угол завернуть

Сердца – за тот за острый
Угол – громов магнит!
Чтобы сердечный остров
Со всех сторон омыт

Kafel... Somewhere, in a peacock's
Mantle, a tower called Eiffel.

To a child, a river is pebbles.
A far piece? No, an orange piece.

In a child's stringed, inmost memory
Distance is hand luggage and a governess.

Not giving it away (Distance is stylish),
What they're dragging along on the carts...

Distance made into a pencil-case...
Corridors: the canals of houses.

Weddings, fates, events, deadlines –
Corridors: the inlets of houses.

Not only brooms walk the corridor
At 5 a.m., with an anonymous letter.

The smell of caraway seeds and turf.
Occupation? Corridor boy.

Claiming only our fair share:
The carmagnole of the corridors.

He who built (dug) the corridors
Knew where to curve them –
To give the blood time
To turn the corner

Of the heart – that acute
Angle is the thunder's magnet:
To wash the heart-isle with blood
From every side.

Был. Коридор сей создан
Мной – не проси ясней! –
Чтобы дать время мозгу
Оповестить по всей

Линии – от «посадки
Нету» до узловой
Сердца: «Идет! Бросаться –
Жмурься! А нет – долой

С рельс!» Коридор сей создан
Мной *(не поэт* – спроста!),
Чтобы дать время мозгу
Распределить места,

Ибо свиданье – местность,
Роспись – подсчет – чертеж –
Слов, не всегда уместных,
Жестов, погрешных сплошь.

Чтобы любовь в порядке –
Вся, чтоб тебе люба –
Вся, до последней складки –
Губ или платья? Лба.

Платье все оправлять умели!
Коридоры: домов туннели.

Точно старец, ведомый дщерью –
Коридоры: домов ущелья.

Друг, гляди! Как в письме, как в сне том –
Это *я* на тебя просветом!

В первом сне, когда веки спустишь –
Это *я* на тебя предчувствьем

The corridor created
By me – don't make me explain!
To give the brain time
To announce over all

The wires – "No further boarding."
And, at the heart-junction: "It's coming!
If you're going to jump – shut your eyes!
If not – keep clear of

The rails!" This corridor created
By me (*Not as a poet* – simply!)
To give the brain time
To assign seats,

For a rendezvous is – a location,
A signature – a calculation – a draft –
Of words often out of place,
Gestures thoroughly false.

So that love may be well,
So that you may love me whole,
Down to the tiniest crease
Of lips, or of dress? – Of brow.

Smoothing out a dress – anyone can do that!
Corridors: the tunnels of houses.

Like an old man led by his daughter –
Corridors: the ravines of houses.

Friend, look: like a letter, like that dream:
I watch you through a ray of hope.

In your first sleep, when you shut your eyelids:
I look at you through a premonition

Света. В крайнюю точку срока
Это *я* – световое око.

А потом?
Сон есть: в тон.
Был – подъем,
Был – наклон
Лба – и лба.
Твой – вперед

Лоб. Груба
Рифма: рот.

Оттого ль, что не стало стен –
Потолок достоверно крен

Дал. Лишь звательный цвел падеж
В ртах. А пол – достоверно брешь.

А сквозь брешь, зелена как Нил...
Потолок достоверно плыл.

Пол же – что, кроме «провались!» –
Полу? Что нам ДО половиц

Сорных? Мало мела? – Горé!
Весь поэт на одном тире

Держится...
        Над *ничем* двух тел
Потолок достоверно пел –

Всеми ангелами.

St. Gilles-sur-Vie,
6-го июня 1926 г.

Of light. Into time's farthest point:
I am the eye of the light.

And what then?
The dream is: unison.
There was a rising.
There was a bending

Of brow to brow.
In front – your brow.

"Brow" – the rhyme is
Crude: "mouth."

Maybe because the walls were gone,
The ceiling definitely gave

A lurch. In our mouths only the vocative
Blossomed. The floor was definitely a gap.

And seen through that gap – green as the Nile…
The ceiling was definitely adrift.

While the floor – what else could we say to the floor
But "Be damned!" What matter the dirty

Boards? Dusty enough? Higher!
By a single dash is the poet held

Together…
　　　　　Over the nothingness of two bodies
The ceiling definitely sang
Like all the angels.

St. Gilles-sur-Vie, 1926

НОВОГОДНЕЕ

С Новым годом – светом – краем – кровом!
Первое письмо тебе на новом
– Недоразумение, что злачном –
(Злачном – жвачном) месте зычном, месте звучном
Как Эолова пустая башня.
Первое письмо тебе с вчерашней,
На которой без тебя изноюсь,
Родины, теперь уже с одной из
Звезд... Закон отхода и отбоя,
По которому любимая любою
И небывшею из небывалой.
Рассказать как про твою узнала?
Не землетрясенье, не лавина.
Человек вошел – любой – (любимый –
Ты). – Прискорбнейшее из событий.
– В Новостях и в Днях. – Статью дадите?
– Где? – В горах. (Окно в еловых ветках.
Простыня.) – Не видите газет ведь?
Так статью? – Нет. – Но... – Прошу избавить.
Вслух: трудна. Внутрь: не христопродавец.
– В санатории. (В раю наемном).
– День? – Вчера, позавчера, не помню.
В Альказаре будете? – Не буду.
Вслух: семья. Внутрь: **всё**, но не Иуда.

С наступающим! (Рождался завтра!) –
Рассказать, что сделала узнав про...?
Тсс... Оговорилась. По привычке.
Жизнь и смерть давно беру в кавычки,
Как заведомо-пустые сплёты,

Ничего не сделала, но что-то
Сделалось, без тени и без эха
Делающее!

NEW YEAR'S GREETINGS

Happy New Year, new sphere, world, home!
My first letter to you in your new
– Not exactly roomy –
(Roomy-ruminant) place: hollow, resonant,
Like the empty tower of Aeolus.
My first letter to you from your one-time motherland
Where without you I shall be heartsick,
A land now already just one of the stars
To you... The law of departure and retreat
By which a cherished lover becomes just another
Face, and the unforgettable becomes the unfeasible.
Shall I tell you how I heard about it?
There was no earthquake, no avalanche.
Someone walked in – no one special (not loved
As you are). "The saddest thing.
It's in The News and in Days. – Will you write us a piece?"
"Where?" "In the mountains." (Fir twigs in a window.
A bedsheet.) "Don't you read the papers?...
So will you write it?" "No." "But..." "Spare me."
Aloud: "It's too hard." Inside: "I'm not a traitor."

"In a sanatorium." (In a rented heaven.)
"When?" "Can't remember – yesterday, or the day before.
Will you be at the Alcázar?" "No."
Aloud: "With family." Inside: "Anything but a Judas."
Happy New One! (You were born tomorrow!)
Shall I tell you what I did when I heard of your...?
Shh... A slip of the tongue. My old habit
Of setting both life and death in quotes
Like so much obviously empty talk.
I did nothing, but something was done,
Something that moves with no echo or
Shadow!

            Теперь – как ехал?
Как рвалось и не разорвалось как –
Сердце? Как на рысаках орловских,
От орлов, сказал, не отстающих,
Дух захватывало – или пуще?
Слаще? Ни высот тому, ни спусков,
На орлах летал заправских русских –
Кто. Связь кровная у нас с тем светом:
На Руси бывал – тот свет на этом
Зрел. Налаженная перебежка!
Жизнь и смерть произношу с усмешкой
Скрытою – своей ея коснешься!
Жизнь и смерть произношу со сноской,
Звездочкою (ночь, которой чаю:
Вместо мозгового полушарья –
Звездное!)
            Не позабыть бы, друг мой,
Следующего: что если буквы
Русские пошли взамен немецких –
То не потому, что нынче, дескать,
Всё сойдет, что мертвый (нищий) всё съест –
Не сморгнет! – а потому что *тот* свет,
Наш, – тринадцати, в Новодевичьем
Поняла: не без- а все-язычен.

Вот и спрашиваю не без грусти:
Уж не спрашиваешь, как по-русски
Nest? Единственная, и все гнезда
Покрывающая рифма: звезды.

Отвлекаюсь? Но такой и вещи
Не найдется – от тебя отвлечься.
Каждый помысел, любой, Du Lieber,
Слог в тебя ведет – о чем бы ни был
Толк (пусть русского родней немецкий
Мне, всех ангельский родней!) – как места
Несть, где нет тебя, нет есть: могила.

    Now, tell me, how was the trip?
How was it, when your heart broke but
Didn't burst? Like riding Orlov trotters,
– Swift as eagles, you said –
Knocking the wind out of you? Or – swifter?
Sweeter? There are neither heights nor
Slopes for one who has flown
On true Russian eagles. We have blood ties
With the beyond. Whoever has been to Russia
Has beheld that world in this. A smooth passage!
I speak of "life" and "death" with a hidden
Smirk (touched with your own smile!).
I say "life" and "death" with a footnote,
With an asterisk (like the night I long for:
Instead of a cerebral hemisphere –
A starry one).
    My friend, let's not forget
The following: if Russian
Letters replace the German ones,
It's not because anything goes now, as they say,
And a dead man (beggar) would swallow anything
Without batting an eye. But because that world, ours,
– This dawned on me when I was thirteen, in Novodevichy –
Is not void of language, but understands each one.

So I ask, not without sadness:
Why do you no longer ask what's the Russian for
"Nest"? There's one rhyme for all havens:
Heaven.

Am I straying from the point? There can be no
Wandering away from you.
Every thought and syllable, Du Lieber,
Leads to you, no matter the topic
(Though German's dearer to me than Russian,
Angelic is dearer still!) – and there's no place
Where you are not, except one: the grave.

Все как не было и все как было,
– Неужели обо мне ничуть не? –
Окруженье, Райнер, самочувствье?
Настоятельно, всенепременно –
Первое видение вселенной
(Подразумевается, поэта
В оной) и последнее – планеты,
Раз только тебе и данной – в целом!
Не поэта с прахом, духа с телом,
(Обособить – оскорбить обоих)
А тебя с тобой, тебя с тобою ж,
– Быть Зевесовым не значит лучшим –
Кастора – тебя с тобой – Поллуксом,
Мрамора – тебя с тобою, травкой,
Не разлуку и не встречу – ставку
Очную: и встречу и разлуку
Первую.   На собственную руку
Как глядел (на след – на ней – чернильный)
Со своей столько-то (сколько?) мильной
Бесконечной ибо безначальной
Высоты над уровнем хрустальным
Средиземного – и прочих блюдец.
Все как не было и все как будет
И со мною за концом предместья.
Все как не было и все как есть уж
– Что списавшемуся до недельки
Лишней! – и куда ж *еще* глядеть-то,
Приоблокотясь на обод ложи,
С этого – как не на тот, с того же
Как не на многострадальный этот.
В Беллевю живу. Из гнезд и веток
Городок. Переглянувшись с гидом:
Беллевю. Острог с прекрасным видом
На Париж – чертог химеры галльской –
На Париж – и на немножко дальше...
Приоблокотясь на алый обод

All as it wasn't, yet all as it was.
– Don't you… at all, about me?…
What is it like, Rainer, how do you feel?
Urgently, without fail –
Your first vision of the universe
(Read: of the poet in it)
And your last – of our planet
Given to you just this once as a whole.
Not as poet and ashes, body and spirit
(To separate them is to offend both)
But a vision of you with you, with yourself,
– Being Zeusian doesn't mean being the best –
Meeting yourself: like Castor and Pollux,
Meeting yourself: like a marble statue meets the grass,
Neither parting nor meeting, but a confrontation
First meeting and first parting.
                    How you looked at your hand,
And at the ink stain on it
From your how many miles
– Infinite because beginningless –
Of height over the crystal plane
Of the Mediterranean – and other saucers.
All as it wasn't, all as it will be
For me too, out beyond the suburbs.
All as it wasn't and all as it already is
– What's an extra week to one who's been written out?
And what else is there to stare at,
Leaning on the edge of a theatre box,
In this life, if not that one, and from that
What but the long-suffering this one.
I live in Bellevue. A town of
Nests and branches. Exchanging glances with the guide:
Bellevue. A prison with a lovely view
Of Paris – a palace of Gallic fancy
Paris – and a bit beyond…
As you lean over that scarlet rim

Как тебе смешны (кому) «должно быть»,
(Мне ж) *должны* быть, с высоты без меры,
Наши Беллевю и Бельведеры!

Перебрасываюсь. Частность. Срочность.
Новый Год в дверях. За что, с кем чокнусь
Через стол? Чем? Вместо пены – ваты
Клок. Зачем? Ну, бьет – а при чем я тут?
Что мне делать в новогоднем шуме
С этой внутреннею рифмой: Райнер – умер.
Если ты, такое око смерклось,
Значит жизнь не жизнь есть, смерть не смерть есть.
Значит – тмится, допойму при встрече! –
Нет ни жизни, нет ни смерти, – третье,
Новое. И за него (соломой
Застелив седьмой – двадцать шестому
Отходящему – какое счастье
Тобой кончиться, тобой начаться!)
Через стол, необозримый оком,
Буду чокаться с тобою тихим чоком
Сткла о сткло? Нет – не кабацким ихним:
Я о *ты*, слиясь дающих рифму:
Третье.
      Через стол гляжу на крест твой.
Сколько мест – загородных, и места
За городом! и кому же машет
Как не нам – куст? Мест – именно наших
И ничьих других! Весь лист! Вся хвоя!
Мест твоих со мной (твоих с тобою).
(Что с тобою бы и на массовку –
Говорить?) что – мест! а месяцов-то!
А недель! А дождевых предместий
Без людей! А утр! А всего вместе
И не начатого соловьями!

Верно плохо вижу, ибо в яме,
Верно лучше видишь, ибо свыше:

How droll they "must seem" to you,
In your immeasurable heights,
Our Bellevues and Belvederes!

    Skip the details. Move on. Urgent.
The New Year's at the door. Who shall I drink with and what?
And to what? Instead of foam, a cotton wad.
What good is it? It's striking twelve. Let it.
In the din of New Year's what am I to do with this
Internal rhyme: "Rainer died"?
If you, if such an eye can be put out,
Then life's not life and death's not death.
It implies – I'll understand this fully when we meet –
Neither life, nor death but a third, something
New… And (keeping the twenty-seventh under straw:
What joy for the twenty-sixth to start and end with you)
Across a vast table unfathomable to the eye,
Shall we toast each other with a quiet clink
Of glass on glass? Not bar-room style:
The clink of "I" on "You,"
To rhyme with the third, the true.
    Over that table I look at your cross.
So many places outside the city, so much space!
To whom does that bush wave
If not to us? These places are ours,
No one else's. All the leaves! All the pine needles!
Places of ours: of you and me (of you and you).
(Here, even on a group outing,
We'd talk?) Places? Whole weeks!
Months! Rainy countryside, with no one
In sight. And the mornings! All this,
Not even begun by the nightingales!

Doubtless, I see poorly from my pit.
Doubtless, you see better from up there.

Ничего у нас с тобой не вышло.
До того, так чисто и так просто
Ничего, так по плечу и росту
Нам – что и перечислять не надо.
Ничего, кроме – не жди из ряду
Выходящего, (неправ из такта
Выходящий!) – а в какой бы, как бы
Ряд вошедшего б?
     Припев извечный:
Ничего хоть чем-нибудь на нечто
Что-нибудь – хоть издали бы – тень хоть
Тени! Ничего, что: час тот, день тот,
Дом тот – даже смертнику в колодках
Памятью дарованное: рот тот!
Или слишком разбирались в средствах?
Из всего *того* один лишь *свет* тот
Наш был, как мы сами только отсвет
Нас, – взамен всего сего – весь *тот* свет!

С незастроеннейшей из окраин –
С новым местом, Райнер, светом, Райнер!
С доказуемости мысом крайним –
С новым оком, Райнер, слухом, Райнер!

Всё тебе помехой
Было: страсть и друг.
С новым звуком, Эхо!
С новым эхом, Звук!

Сколько раз на школьном табурете:
Что за горы там? Какие реки?
Хороши ландшафты без туристов?
Не ошиблась, Райнер – рай – гористый,
Грозовой? Не притязаний вдовьих –
Не один ведь рай, над ним другой ведь
Рай? Террасами? Сужу по Татрам –
Рай не может не амфитеатром

Nothing came of it between us.
So simply and so purely nothing,
So well befitting our stature and strength,
That there's no need to recount it.
Nothing, except: don't expect anything out
Of the ordinary – out of line (the one who falls
Out of step is wrong!) And what other
Line and how could you fall in?
                                        The old refrain:
Though there's nothing – even if nothing…
Oh, let it be something, even if from afar, even
The shadow of a shade! Nothing: that hour, that day,
That house. Even a condemned man, in chains,
Is entitled to memory's gift: that mouth!
Or have we been too choosy?
Of all that, only that world
Was ours, as we are only a reflection of
Ourselves; in place of all this we have all of that world.

To the least built-up-outpost –
Happy new place! Happy new realm, Rainer!
To the farthest cape of the provable –
Happy new sight! Happy new hearing, Rainer!

Everything was a hindrance to you:
Even passion, even friends.
Happy new sound, Echo!
Happy new echo, Sound!

How often, at the classroom desk:
What mountains are there? What rivers?
Are they lovely, landscapes without tourists?
Was I right, Rainer – is heaven mountainous,
Thunderous? Not just the heaven of widows' claims –
There's not just one heaven, above it
Another one? With terraces? Judging by the Tatras –
Heaven must be an amphitheatre.

Быть. (А занавес над кем-то спущен...)
Не ошиблась, Райнер, Бог – *растущий*
Баобаб? Не Золотой Людовик –
Не один ведь Бог? Над ним другой ведь
Бог?

      Как пишется на новом месте?
Впрочем *есть* ты – *есть* стих: сам и есть ты –
Стих! Как пишется в хорошей жисти
Без стола для локтя, лба для кисти
(Горсти).

      – Весточку, привычным шифром!
Райнер, радуешься новым рифмам?
Ибо правильно толкуя слово
Рифма – что – как не – целый ряд новых
Рифм – Смерть?

      Некуда: язык изучен.
Целый ряд значений и созвучий
Новых.

      – До свиданья! До знакомства!
Свидимся – не знаю, но – споемся.
С мне-самой неведомой землею –
С целым морем, Райнер, с целой мною!

Не разъехаться – черкни заране.
С новым звукопачертаньем, Райнер!

В небе лестница, по ней с Дарами...
С новым рукоположеньем, Райнер!

– Чтоб не залили держу ладонью. –
Поверх Роны и поверх Rarogn'a,
Поверх явной и сплошной разлуки
Райнеру – Мария – Рильке – в руки.

BELLEVUE, 7-го ФЕВРАЛЯ 1927 г.

(The curtain falls on someone…)
So was I right, Rainer, is God a growing
Baobab? Not a Gold Louis –
Not just one God? Above him – another
God?
      How's your writing in the new place?
Though if you're there, poetry is: you yourself are
Poetry. How's your writing in that good life
With no desk for your elbow, no forehead
For your palm?
              – Write me a note, in our usual code.
Pleased with the new rhymes, Rainer?
Since – what's the meaning of the word,
But a whole new range of rhymes:
Death?
      Impasse: the tongue's been mastered.
A whole range of new meanings and new
Assonances.
          – Till we meet! Till we are reacquainted!
I don't know if we'll meet but we will sing together.
Here's to your new world still unknown to me,
Here's to the whole sea, Rainer, to the whole me!

So we don't pass like ships – scribble a line.
Happy new tracing of sounds, Rainer!

A ladder in heaven – there, gift-laden, climbing…
Happy new placing of hands, Rainer!

I cup my eyes, so that nothing will spill.
Across the Rhone and across the Rarogne,
Across the sure and final parting's land,
Put this into Rainer Maria Rilke's hand.

BELLEVUE, 7 FEBRUARY 1927

ПОЭМА ВОЗДУХА

Ну, вот и двустишье
Начальное. Первый гвоздь.
Дверь явно затихла,
Как дверь, за которой гость.
Стоявший – так хвоя
У входа, спросите вдов –
Был полон покоя,
Как гость, за которым зов
Хозяина, бденье
Хозяйское. Скажем так:
Был полон терпенья,
Как гость, за которым знак
Хозяйки – всей тьмы знак! –
Та молния поверх слуг!
Живой или призрак –
Как гость, за которым стук
Сплошной, не по средствам
Ничьим – оттого и мрем –
Хозяйкина сердца:
Березы под топором.
(Расколотый ящик
Пандорин, ларец забот!)
Без счету – входящих,
Но кто же без стука – ждет?
Уверенность в слухе
И в сроке. Припав к стене,
Уверенность в ухе
Ответном. (Твоя – во мне.)
Заведомость входа.
Та сладкая (игры в страх!)
Особого рода
Оттяжка – с ключом в руках.
Презрение к чувствам,
Над миром мужей и жен –
Та Оптина пустынь,

POEM OF THE AIR

So, here is the opening couplet,
The first nail driven in.
The door is noticeably still,
As if a guest were behind it.
The stationary guest (like a pine
At the door – ask any widow)
Was serene,
Like a guest who has earned
His host's invitation, his host's
Attentions. Put it this way:
He was patient
Like a guest under the sign
Of his hostess – pitch darkness –
A flash of lightning over the servants!
Man or spectre – a guest
Followed by the endless knocking no one
Can put up with; and so
The hostess's heart sinks
Like a birch under the axe
(Pandora's box split open,
A coffer-full of troubles).
Those entering are countless,
But who, without knocking, waits?
With faith in hearing and time,
And, pressing against the wall,
Faith in the responsive ear
(Echoing your faith in me).
The certainty of an entrance,
A certain sweet lingering
(Playing at fear!) –
Key in hand.
Contempt for feelings;
Over the world of husbands and wives,
A monastery like Optin

Отдавшая – даже звон.
Душа без прослойки
Чувств. Голая, как феллах.
Дверь делала стойку.
Не то же ли об ушах?
Как фавновы рожки
Вставали. Как ро–та... пли!
Еще бы немножко –
Да просто сошла б с петли
От силы присутствья
Заспинного. В час страстей
Так жилы трясутся,
 Натянутые сверх всей
Возможности. Стука
Не следовало. Пол – плыл.
Дверь кинулась в руку.
Мрак – чуточку отступил.

§

Полная естественность.
Свойственность. Застой.
Лестница, как лестница,
Час, как час (ночной).
Вдоль стены распластанность
Чья-то. Одышав
Садом, кто-то явственно
Уступал мне шаг –
В полную божественность
Ночи, в полный рост Неба.
(Точно лиственниц
Шум, пены о мост...)
В полную неведомость
Часа и страны.
В полную невидимость
Даже на тени.

That renounced even the chiming of bells.
Soul without stratum
Of feelings; naked as a fellah.
The door stood upside down;
And didn't the ears as well?
They stood up like a faun's
Horns; like a squadron – fire!
Any more, and the door
Would have come unhinged
From the force of the presence
Behind it! Thus, in the hour of passion,
Stretched beyond all possibility,
Blood vessels throb. No knocking
Followed. The floor drifted.
The door jumped into my hand.
Gradually the darkness stepped aside.

§

Total artlessness.
Lack of constraint. Slumber.
A typical staircase,
A typical hour (night).
Someone sprawling along the
Wall. Exhaling
The garden smells, someone was definitely
Letting me have the first step –
In night's
Full divinity,
The full height of the sky.
(Like the hum of a larch, or of
White water swashing a bridge…)
In complete ignorance
Of time and place;
Complete invisibility,
Even in shade.
(The night's no longer pitch black

(Не черным-черна уже
Ночь, черна – черным!
Оболочки радужной
Киноварь, кармин –
Расцепив сетчаткою
Мир на сей и твой –
Больше не запачкаю
Ока – красотой.)
Сон? Но, в лучшем случае –
Слог. А в нем? под ним?
Чудится? Дай вслушаюсь:
Мы, а шаг один!
И не парный, слаженный,
Тот, сиротство двух.
Одиночный – каждого
Шаг – пока не дух:
Мой. (Не то, что дыры в них –
Стыд, а вот – платать!)
Что-то нужно выравнять:
Либо ты на пядь
Снизься, на мыслителей
Всех – державу всю!
Либо – и услышана:
Больше не звучу.

Полная срифмованность.
Ритм, впервые мой!
Как Колумб здороваюсь
С новою землей –
Воздухом. Ходячие
Истины забудь!
С сильною отдачею
Грунт, как будто грудь
Женщины под стоптанным
Вое-сапогом.
(Матери под стопками
Детскими...)

140

In this absolute blackness.
The iris of the eye is cinnabar and carmine…
Having filtered the world
– Into yours and everyone else's –
Through the retina,
I will no longer tarnish
This eye with beauty.)
A dream? No. At best –
A mode. And in it? Under it?
Or does it only seem that way? Listen:
We, but a single footstep!
Not the conjugal, coordinated
Pace of paired orphans,
But the individual step of each;
Still not a spirit,
Mine.
(Not that they're torn – shame!
But still we have to mend them.)
Something has to be levelled:
Either you come down an inch
To all thinkers –
The whole kingdom! –
Or, even if I'm heard,
I no longer sound.

A perfect rhyme pattern.
Rhythm, mine for the first time!
Like Columbus, I greet
This new land –
The air. Forget worn-out
Truths. This soil springs back
Firmly, like a woman's
Breast, under a worn-out
Soldier's boot.
(Mother's breast under children's
Feet…)
        Stepping

		В тугом
Шаг. Противу – мнения:
Не удобохож
Путь. Сопротивлением
Сферы, как сквозь рожь
Русскую, сквозь отроду
Рис, – тобой, Китай!
Словно моря противу
(Противу: читай –
По сердцу!) сплечением
Толп. – Гераклом бьюсь!
– Землеизлучение.
Первый воздух – густ.

Сню тебя иль снюсь тебе, –
Сушь, вопрос седин
Лекторских.
Дай, вчувствуюсь:
Мы, а вздох один!
И не парный, спаренный,
Тот, удушье двух, –
Одиночной камеры
Вздох: еще не взбух
Днепр? Еврея с цитрою
Вэрыд: ужель оглох?
Что-то нужно выправить:
Либо ты на вздох
Сдайся, на всесушие
Все, – страшась прошу –
Либо – и отпущена:
Больше не дышу.

Времечко осадное,
То, сыпняк в Москве!
Кончено. Отстрадано
В каменном мешке
Легкого! Исследуйте
Слизь! Сняты врата

Through dense substance.
Against the current.
This road is not easy
To tread. Pushing through air:
Like wading through Russian rye,
Through miracle-rice,
And through you, China!
As though challenging the sea,
(Challenging means
Obeying the heart) with the throng's
Joined shoulders. – I fight like a Hercules.
– Earthradiance.
The first air is dense.

I dream you, or you of me,
A question fit for professorial
Greyness. Let me feel my way in:
We, but a single sigh,
And not that conjugal, coupled sigh,
The asphyxia of both, –
The sigh of solitary
Confinement: "Hasn't the Dnieper
Spilled over yet?" The wail of a Jew
With a zither: "Have I grown deaf?"
Something to put right:
Either you yield up
A sigh
To the living – I fearfully ask –
Or, even if freed,
I no longer breathe.

The time of the siege,
That one! Typhus in Moscow.
Finished… It was suffered through
In the stone bag
Of the lung. Inspect
The mucus. The gates of air

Воздуха. Оседлости
Прорвана черта.

Мать! Недаром чаяла:
Цел воздухобор!
Но сплошное аэро —
Сам — зачем прибор?
Твердь, стелись под лодкою
Леткою — утла!
Но — сплошное легкое —
Сам — зачем петля
Мертвая? Полощется...
Плещется... И вот —
Не жалейте летчика!
Тут-то и полет!
Не рядите в саваны
Косточки его.
Курс воздухоплаванья —
Смерть, и ничего
Нового в ней. (Розысков
Дичь... Щепы?... Винты?...)
Ахиллесы воздуха
— Все! — хотя б и *ты*,
Не дышите славою,
Воздухом низов.
Курс воздухоплаванья —
Смерть, где все с азов,
Заново...

Слава тебе, допустившему бреши:
Больше не вешу.
Слава тебе, обвалившему крышу:
Больше не слышу.
Солнцепричастная, больше не щурюсь.
Дух: не дышу уж!
Твердое тело есть мертвое тело:
Оттяготела,

Are lifted; the pale
Of settlement, wrecked.

Mother! You'd seen it coming:
The Air-Warrior is still alive.
But why the sheer air
Itself – a tool?
Firmament, spread yourself
Under the winged boat: it's frail.
But why the sheer lightness –
Itself – a fatal
Noose? Flailing…
Flapping… Now –
Do not pity the pilot.
Now is the flight.
Do not dress
His bones in a shroud.
The course of aeronautics
Is death, nothing
New in it. (The farce of
A search… Wreckage? Shards?)
Every Achilles of the air –
Everyone! – even *you* –
Do not breathe glory,
The air of lower depths.
The course of aeronautics
Is death, where all
Begins anew…

Glory to you, who overlooked a crack:
I weigh nothing.
Glory to you, who made the roof fall:
I no longer hear.
Sun-merged, I no longer squint.
A spirit, I breathe no longer.
The solid body is a dead body:
Gravity is gone.

Легче, легче лодок
На слюде прибрежий.
О, как воздух легок:
Реже – реже – реже...
Баловливых рыбок
Скользь – форель за кончик...
О, как воздух ливок,
Ливок! Ливче гончей
Сквозь овсы, а скользок!
Волоски – а веек! –
Тех, что только ползать
Стали – ливче леек!
Что я – скользче лыка
Свежего, и лука.
Пагодо-музыкой
Бусин и бамбука, –
Пагодо-завесой...
Плещь! Все шли б и шли бы...
Для чего Гермесу –
Крыльца? Плавнички бы –
Пловче! Да ведь ливмя
Льет! Ирида! Ирис!
Не твоим ли ливнем
Шемахинским или ж
Кашемирским...
                  Танец –
Ввысь! Таков от клиник
Путь: сперва не тянет
Персть, потом не примет
Ног. Без дна, а тверже
Льдов! Закон отсутствий
Всех: сперва не держит
Твердь, потом не пустит
В вес. Наяда? Пэри?
Баба с огорода!
Старая потеря
Тела через воду

Lighter, lighter than the boats
On the seashore mica,
O how light is the air:
Thinner – thinner – thinner…
The gliding of playful fishes –
A trout swims by…
O how the air flows,
How it streams! Flowing as a hound
Through oat stalks, gliding;
Hair – thin, blowing;
More teeming
Than the newly crawling;
More slippery
Than fibres and leeks.
Flowing with pagoda-music
Of beads and bamboo –
A pagoda's shutters…
Splash! And still going…
Why wings for Hermes?
Fins: better for swimming. Torrents;
It's pouring rain. Iris! Irida!
Isn't this your Shemakhan or Kashmir
Cloudburst…
    A dance –
Upwards! This is the way
Out of the sickroom:
First, your fingers
Lose their grip, then the legs…
Bottomless, yet harder than
Ice! The law of all absences:
First the firmament
Refuses to hold you,
Then you're not allowed
The weight. Naiad? Nymph?
No, a wife from a kitchen-garden!
The ancient loss
Of body to water

(Водо-сомущения
Плеск. Песчаный спуск...)
– Землеотпущение.
Третий воздух – пуст.

§

Седью, как сквозь невод
Дедов, как сквозь косу
Бабкину, – а редок!
Редок, реже проса
В засуху. (Облезут
Все, верхи бесхлебны.)
О, как воздух резок,
Резок, реже гребня
Песьего, для песьих
Курч. Счастливых засек
Редью. Как сквозь просып
Первый (нам-то – засып!)
Бредопереездов
Редь, связать-неможность.
О, как воздух резок,
Резок, резче ножниц.
Нет, резца... Как жальцем
В боль – уже на убыль.
Репью, как сквозь пальцы...
Сердца, как сквозь зубы
Довода – на Credo
Уст полураскрытых.
О, как воздух цепок,
Цепок, цедче сита
Творческого (влажен
Ил, бессмертье – сухо).
Цедок, цедче глаза
Гетевского, слуха
Рильковского... (Шепчет
Бог, своей – страшася

(Splash of a waterflurry.
The sandy descent...)
The letting-go-of-the-earth.
The third air is empty.

§

Grey-haired, as seen through an ancestor's
Nets, or a grandmother's
Tresses – it's rarefied.
Rarefied: thinner than millet
In a drought (they'll all grow thin,
Their tops barren.)
How harsh the air is,
How sharp: sharper than a
Comb made for a cur's
Curls. It's the air's thinness
That kills happy folk. As though
Within the first sleep-through
(Their sound sleep – our just dropping off)
Of delirious crossings –
A thinness not-to-be-tied.
O how sharp the air is,
Sharper than scissors –
Or chisel... A sting
Into pain, already subsiding.
Thinness seeping through fingers...
Of the heart, as through the clenched teeth
Of argument – onto the Credo
Of half-open lips.
How filtering the air is,
More so than a creator's
Sieve (silt is moist, immortality – dry);
More so than Goethe's eye,
Rilke's hearing... (God
Whispers, fearful of his own
Might...)

Мощи...)
　　　　А не цедче
Разве только часа
Судного...
　　　　В ломоту
Жатв – зачем рождаем...
Всем неумолотом,
Всем неурожаем
Верха... По расщелинам
Сим – ни вол ни плуг.
– Землеотлучение:
Пятый воздух – звук.

§

Голубиных грудок
Гром – отсюда родом!
О, как воздух гудок,
Гудок, гудче года
Нового! Порубок
Гуд, дубов под корень.
О, как воздух гудок,
Гудок, гудче горя
Нового, спасиба
Царского... Под градом
Жести, гудче глыбы –
В деле, гудче клада –
В песне, в большеротой
Памяти народной.
Соловьиных глоток
Гром – отсюда родом!
Рыдью, медью, гудью,
Вьюго-Богослова
Гудью – точно грудью
Певчей – небосвода
Небом или лоном
Лиро-черепахи?

　　　　Only not more filtering, maybe,
Than the hour of
Judgement...
　　　　Why bear children
Into the ache of the harvest?...
Into all the unmilled,
Into all the failed crops of
Heights... Neither ox,
Nor plough enters these clefts.
– Excommunication-from-the-earth.
The fifth air is sound.

§

The thunder
Of doves' breasts starts here.
How the air hums,
More resonant
Than the New
Year – the hum of an oak-thicket,
Illegally cut at the roots.
How the air hums,
More resonant than a new sorrow
Drones, or a tsar' s
Thankyous... Under the tin avalanche
More resonant than a boulder rolling, than treasure
In a song, in the wide-mouthed
Folk memory. The thunder
Of nightingales' throats starts here.
Sobbing, copper-like hum
Of a Snow-Seminarian
– A singer's chest;
The heavenly vault of a palate,
Or the back of a lyre-turtle?
More resonant than the Don
In battle, than the headsman's block
A-harvesting... Down inclines

151

Гудок, гудче Дона
В битву, гудче плахи
В жатву... По загибам,
Погрознее горных,
Звука, как по глыбам
Фив нерукотворных.
Семь – пласты и зыби!
Семь – heilige Sieben!
Семь в основе лиры,
Семь в основе мира.
Раз основа лиры –
Семь, основа мира –
Лирика. Так глыбы
Фив по звуку лиры...
О, еще в котельной
Тела – «легче пуха!»
Старая потеря
Тела через ухо.
Ухом – чистым духом
Быть. Оставьте буквы –
Веку.
            Чистым слухом
Или чистым звуком
Движемся? Преднота
Сна. Предзноб блаженства.
Гудок, гудче грота
В бури равноденствья.
Темени – в падучке,
Голода – утробой
Гудче... А не гудче
Разве только гроба
В Пасху...
           И гудче гудкого –
Паузами, промежутками
Мочи, и движче движкого –
Паузами, передышками
Паровика за мучкою...

More daunting than mountain ones,
Down the curves of sound as if down the
Blocks of Thebes not of human making.
Seven – layers and ripplings.
Seven – heilige Sieben.
Seven – the base of the lyre.
Seven – the base of the world.
If the base of the lyre is
Seven, then the base of the world
Is lyric. Thus the Theban
Clods followed the voice of the lyre…
O, yet in the boiler-house,
Bodies, "light as a feather."
The ancient loss
Of flesh to the ear.
To become pure spirit
Through the unfaltering ear.
Leave the letters to time. Is it pure ear
Or pure sound that moves the world? The grace-note
Before sleep. The first throb of bliss.
More resonant than a grotto
In an equinoctial storm,
Than the cranium in an epileptic fit,
Than the stomach
In hunger… But not more resonant
Than a coffin at Easter…
      And even more resonant
In its pauses, intervals
Of might; and even more movable
In its pauses, a steam-engine's
Stopping for flour…
Through the interchange
Of the best divine gestures:
Of air with better-than-air.
And I can't say those are sweet
Pauses: they are transfers
From the local to the interspatial –

Чередованьем лучшего
Из мановений божеских:
Воздуха с – лучше-воздуха!
И – не скажу, чтоб сладкими –
Паузами: пересадками
С местного в межпространственный –
Паузами, полустанками
Сердца, когда от легкого –
Ох! – полуостановками
Вздоха – мытарства рыбного
Паузами, перерывами
Тока, паров на убыли
Паузами, перерубами
Пульса, – невнятно сказано:
Паузами – ложь, раз *спазмами* –
Вздоха ... Дыра бездонная
Легкого, пораженного
Вечностью...
              Не все ее –
Так. Иные – смерть.
– Землеотсечение.
Кончен воздух. Твердь.

Музыка надсадная!
Вздох, всегда вотще!
Кончено! Отстрадано
В газовом мешке
Воздуха. Без компаса
Ввысь! Дитя – в отца!
Час, когда потомственность
Ска-зы-ва-ет-ся.
Твердь! Голов бестормозных –
Трахт! И как отсечь:
Полная оторванность
Темени от плеч –
Сброшенных! Беспочвенных –
Грунт! Гермес – свои!

These pauses, respites of the heart
When from the lung:
Ah! – half-stops
Of breath, the pauses
Of fish – afflictions, intermittent
Current, steam subsiding,
Breaks in the pulse – unclearly told,
In pauses: a lie, if it is said,
In gasps… The bottomless hole
Of the lung, struck
With eternity…
                    Not all call it
That. To some it's death.
Severance-of-the-earth.
The air – done. Now – firmament.

Heart-rending music
A sigh, always in vain.
– Done. Suffered out
In the gas bag
Of air. Upwards –
Without a compass! Like father,
Like son. The hour when heredity
Is made manifest.
Firmament. Heads without breaks:
Crash-road. Nothing can sever them:
Complete independence
Of head from shoulders,
Long since shed. The ground
For the un-grounded. At last
We're yours, Hermes! A full, precise
Sense of the winged
Head. There are no two ways.
Only one – straight.
Thus, sucked into space,
The steeple drops the church,
Leaving it to the days. God makes

Полное и точное
Чувство головы
С крыльями. Двух способов
Нет – один и прям.
Так, пространством всосанный,
Шпиль роняет храм –
Дням. Не в день, а исподволь
Бог сквозь дичь и глушь
Чувств. Из лука – выстрелом –
Ввысь! Не в царство душ –
В полное владычество
Лба. Предел? – Осиль:
В час, когда готический
Храм нагонит шпиль
Собственный – и вычислив
Всё, – когорты числ!
В час, когда готический
Шпиль нагонит смысл
Собственный...

Медон, в дни Линдберга.

Himself felt not in a day, but gradually,
Through feelings' dreck
And dregs. A shot from a bow –
Upwards. Not into the kingdom of souls
But into the full self-possession
Of the head. Limits? Conquer them:
The hour when the Gothic
Church overtakes its own
Steeple, – having counted
Them all – the cohorts of numbers!...
The hour when the Gothic
Spire overtakes its own
Intent...

    MEUDON, DURING THE LINDBERGH DAYS

NOTES

On a Red Steed
On a Red Steed is connected to the cycle *The Parting*, which was addressed to Sergei Efron, M.T.'s husband. Its theme is the poet's calling, embodied in the image of the winged Genius for whose sake the poet sacrifices everything, even life itself. Ariadna Efron, M.T.'s daughter, was convinced that the hero of the poem was the "complex, dynamic … image of Alexander Blok whom M.T. idolised, … the pure … Genius of poetry, who dwelled on heights of poetry which M.T. considered inaccessible to herself."

Sorokoust: Russian Orthodox prayers for the deceased. The prayers continue for forty days.

Poem of the Mountain
Like *Poem of the End* which followed it, *Poem of the Mountain* is based on M.T.'s relationship with Konstantin Rodzevich in Prague. At the end of September 1923, in her first notes for the poem, she wrote: "The streets like stairs. Sloping … About Solomon's ring. About Job. Seeing each other off: the whole way. The coffee shop – the embankment – the bridge – the staircase – the mountain – the vacant lot." Also: "There must be a poem of parting … The parting was in the air – with more certainty than the sword of Damocles … He asks for a home, while all she can offer is her soul." M.T. began *Poem of the Mountain* on January 1, 1924 and finished it on February I.

The Mountain is Petrshinsky Hill in Prague where M.T. lived in the fall of 1923. The Mountain is also a symbol of love and genius towering over mundane reality. Throughout the poem, M.T. plays on the similar-sounding Russian words for "mountain" and "grief" ("gora" and "gore").

The epigraph is from Hölderlin's novel *Hyperion, or a Hermit in Greece*: "O beloved! Are you surprised by this speech? All who are parting talk like drunks and love solemnity…"

Each shall be given, according to his tears: this is a paraphrase of the Biblical "to give every man according as his work shall be." (*Revelations* 22:12)

Memento (Lat.): "remember." M.T. is playing on the Latin expression "memento mori" (remember death) and the Russian word for the sea, "more." I tried to come up with an English equivalent of her pun.

The twelve apostles: a reference to the Biblical apostles, and also to the figures which appear on the clock of the Prague town hall whenever the clock strikes.

POEM OF THE END

On January 27, 1974, while still working on *Poem of the Mountain,* M.T. outlined a plan for *Poem of the End,* which at first she called *Poem of the Last Time.* The lovers meet in the city and, as they progress outside of it, the finality of this meeting, their last, becomes clearer and their parting more inevitable. "1. A meeting by a street-lamp. 2. Coffee shop. A window into emptiness. 3. Along the embankment. ... A bridge into infinity. 4. Last streets ... 5. Another street-lamp. 6. The mountain (a fence). 7. The last gesture."

A later outline was more detailed and set out twelve parts, adding one in which the lovers pass a coffee shop they used to sit in when they were in love. The final version of the poem is made up of fourteen "chapters." M.T. began writing *Poem of the End* while completing the final stanzas of *Poem of the Mountain.* Her initial notes for the two poems have some points in common. However, as she wrote to Pasternak on May 26, 1926, "...the Mountain [i.e. *Poem of the Mountain*] was earlier and it was – a man's, an immediate response, on the highest note at once, while *Poem of the End* is a woman's grief, bursting into tears; I, when I lie down – am no longer I when I rise. *Poem of the Mountain* is a mountain as seen from the top of another mountain. *Poem of the End* – the mountain is on me, I'm under it." She finished *Poem of the End* in the Czech village of Ilovišči on July 9, 1924.

...a post: a lamppost. In MT.'s preliminary notes, the first part of the poem was to be summarized above. The first part was to be "a meeting by a streetlamp."

Burning not only with the light of dawn: c.f. a line in a poem by Alexander Blok "...On the last floor, there, under the high roof,/ A window burning not only with the light of dawn..."

Bertold Schwartz: (14th century), considered the inventor of gunpowder.

Lovelace: a hero of Richardson's novel *Clarissa,* the Russian equivalent of a Don Juan.

Like a seal on your heart... words of the Bride from the *Song of Songs*: "Set me as a seal upon thine heart,/ as a seal upon thine arm: for love is strong as death..." (8:6, KJV)

Golcond: a city in India, famous for its diamonds; here it is used as a symbol of plenty.

One of a hundred: this is a pun in Russian. The root of the first-person plural form of "separating" ("ra-stayomsia") sounds like the genitive of the word for "hundred" ("sta").

Khlebnikov, Velimir (1885–1922): a Russian Futurist poet, a great innovator of poetic language.

An Attempt at a Room
This *poema* is addressed to Pasternak and Rilke. In her letter to Pasternak (February 9, 1927), written a day after she completed *New Year's Greetings*, M.T. wrote: "The poem about you and me ... came out as a poem about him and me, every line *of* it. An interesting substitution: the poem was written in the days of my extreme concentration on him, but it was directed – with its will and its conscience – to you. And it came out – not just about him!. ...but about him – now, (after December 29th) [i.e., after Rilke's death], as an anticipation, a foresight. I simply told him, the living, whom I wasn't going to join! ... how we haven't met, how we met differently. That's the reason for the strange ... unlovingness, renunciation, denial in each line. The work was called *An Attempt at a Room,* and with every line – every [attempt] was denied..."

A dispatch, Dno: At the station Dno, on the night of March 1, 1917, the train carrying Tsar Nicolas II to Tsarskoe Selo was stopped and redirected to Pskov, where the tsar abdicated on March 2.

Danzas: Pushkin's second in his fatal duel, see below.

D'Anthès: the Frenchman who killed the poet Pushkin in a duel in 1837. *Cheka:* the Soviet secret police. Wall of the Cheka – a reference to the Communist terror.

Revel: old name for Tallinn, the capital of Estonia.

Grifel (slate-pencil) – *tufel* (shoe) – *kafel* (tile): a set of rhyming words in Russian.

The carmagnole: a song popular during the French revolution.

New Year's Greetings
At Pasternak's request, Rilke sent M.T. his *Duino Elegies* and *Sonnets to Orpheus*. M.T.'s response was: "You're not my most beloved poet – most (beloved) is a degree; you are – a natural phenomenon, ... its incarnate fifth element: poetry itself ... you are – that from which poetry springs and which is more than poetry, than yourself..."

Correspondence with Rilke absorbed M.T. and this is reflected in her narrative poems written in the spring and summer of 1926, *From the Sea* and *An Attempt at a Room*. In their letters the two poets discuss their plans to meet in person. But this was not lo be: Rilke died on December, 29 1926. M.T. was shocked by his death. Having just learned of it, she wrote him a letter in German on December 31. The letter had many points in common with the motives she worked into her long poem *New Year's Greetings*. This long poem, which she finished on February 7, 1927, was for her a continuation of her dialogue with Rilke – she often called it her 'Letter to Rilke.'

M.T. also wrote an essay about Rilke, 'Your Death.' She translated a selection of Rilke's letters to her and had them published in *Volya Rossii*, an émigré journal. In her March 8, 1935 letter to her poet friend Ivask she wrote: "...Of those equal to me in strength I met only Rilke and Pasternak. ... O not only in poetic strength! In total strength plus in poetry (i.e, verbally creative)."

For his part, Rilke is known to have addressed at least three poems to M.T. One was a short poem he inscribed in the copy of *Sonnets to Orpheus* that he sent to M.T. with his first letter. Another one was written on the flyleaf of a copy of his book of French poems, *Vergers*. The third poem was 'Elegy (for Marina Tsvetaeva Efron)', which Rilke sent to M.T. in his letter of 8 June 1926.

... place : the word M.T. uses here ("zlachnom") may be a reference to a Russian Orthodox prayer for the dead: "Gospodi, upokoi dushu raba Tvoego ... v meste svetle, v meste zlachne, v meste pokoine..." In the poem's fourth line M.T. makes a pun ("zlachnom-zhvachnom"). The translation is an attempt to preserve the semblance, if not the literal meaning, of the pun, so that at least its second part has meaning close to M.T.'s ("ruminant" for M.T.'s "zhvachnom").

A person walked in: it was Mark Slonim who told M.T. of Rilke's death.

The News and *Days: (Poslednie Novosti; Dni)* these were the names of the major Russian émigré newspapers.

In a sanatorium: Rilke died on 29 December 1926 in the sanatorium Valmont in Switzerland.

Alcazar: a Paris restaurant. M.T. was invited there for a crowded New Year's party. In the next line, she excuses herself from going ("Family ties"). Anything but a Judas: To her, joining a merry New Year's crowd would amount to a betrayal of Rilke whose death she has just learned of.

Orlov Trotters: this may be a reference to Rilke's poem 'The Night Ride. St. Petersburg' (1907): "Even now, with my own eyes, I see them / those black Orlov trotters..."

161

Novodevichy: a famous old monastery in Moscow.

Nest: The German word is used; its meaning is the same as the English one. Rilke, in one of his letters, asked M.T. what the Russian for "nest" was. Here M.T. offers him the rhyme "zvyozdy" – stars, i.e., eternity.

Du Lieber (Ger.): beloved.

Bellevue (Fr.), *Belvedere* (Ital.): a beautiful view.

Gifts: the bread and wine of the Eucharist.

Rhone: the river which flows into Lake Geneva. Rilke spent his last years there.

Rarogne: the place where Rilke is buried.

Poem of the Air

M.T.'s dating of the poem "during Lindbergh" corresponds to May 20–21, 1927 when Charles Lindbergh made the first solo non-stop transatlantic flight and landed in Paris. In its own way, *Poem of the Air* continues *New Year's Greetings*: Rilke's shade guides the author through the seven heavens, the seven strata of air, into airless space.

Optin: Optina Pustyn, a monastery in pre-Revolutionary Russia, located in Kaluga province.

Have I grown deaf M. Belkina, in her article 'The Lost Notebook', says that M.T. wrote in the margin next to this line: "NB. Meaning: Have I grown deaf? (Implied: God. Because – about what else can a Jew with a zither think?)"

Mother!… The Air-Warrior…: in the margin (see above) M.T. wrote: "NB. This is about Lindbergh who, at that time, flew over the ocean, and about his mother who taught him to renounce all earthly honours and gains. If I remember her name – I'll write it in."

Shemakhan, Kashmir: two kinds of colourful silk rugs, named after the places where they were made. The rainbow (i.e., Iris) in a cloudburst is compared to this colourful silk.

The back of a lyre-turtle: in the Greek myth, Hermes made the first seven-stringed lyre from the shell of a turtle he found by chance. Later, he gave the lyre to Apollo.

Thebes, not human-made: according to one version of the myth, the walls around the city of Thebes were built by Amphion and Zet, the sons of Zeus. Strong Zet carried and piled up the stones, while Amphion played the lyre given to him by Hermes: the beautiful sounds forced the stones to move to the assigned places.

Heilige Sieben (Ger.): the sacred seven. The number seven is considered magical in mythology (and numerology); it is seen as part of the universal order itself: seven notes on the musical scale, seven colours of the rainbow, seven days for each of the four phases of the moon.

…hole of the lung: M. Belkina reports a notation M.T. made in the manuscript of the *poema:* "This *poema* was written as an answer to the question put by Vera Arensky, a clairvoyant sick young woman, Yury Zavadsky's sister: 'Marina, how will I die?'" Thus: The bottomless hole / Of the lung, struck With eternity…This *poema,* like many of my other works, was written – in order to find out." Vera Arensky died of tuberculosis.

Lightning Source UK Ltd.
Milton Keynes UK
UKHW041501141021
392146UK00001B/57

9 781848 617780